D0635781

Personality Fulfillment in the Religious Life

VOLUME ONE

Religious Life in a Time of Transition

by
ADRIAN VAN KAAM, C.S.Sp.

DIMENSION BOOKS
WILKES-BARRE, PA.

Published by Dimension Books
Wilkes-Barre, Pennsylvania

Library of Congress Catalog Card Number: 67-16816
First American Edition 1967 by Dimension Books

Imprimatur:

✠ Most Rev. Vincent M. Leonard, D.D.
Vicar General-Chancellor
May 9, 1967

Nihil Obstat:

William J. Winter, S.T.D.
Censor Librorum
May 8, 1967

Imprimi Potest:

Vernon F. Gallagher, C.S.Sp.
Provincial

CONTENTS

PREFACE

This essay on religious life has been written not from the perspective of theology but from the viewpoint of a newly emerging integrative discipline, *religion and personality* or *religious anthropology*. I have attempted to illuminate the meaning and fundamental structure of the active religious life in the light of insights which have arisen from the integration of social-scientific data and theories relevant to an understanding of man as a religious being. When these findings and hypotheses are assimilated within the specific doctrine and tradition of a religion or denomination, it is clear that their content and formulation will be complemented by the theology concerned. Though a student in this field of pre-theological exploration may suggest possible implications of his findings for a specific area of a certain religion, he cannot assume theological authority for his statements. Such hypothetical suggestions have been made throughout this essay in regard to religious life as lived in accordance with Catholic tradition; however, it is the privilege of the theologian and the authorities in the Church and its religious communities to discover and decide just how much and in what way these pre-theological considerations may or may not be adopted.

Moreover, I have restricted my considerations to the overall meaning of the *active* religious life only, and the implications of this meaning for only two aspects of this life — community structures and community encounter. In a complementary volume, I hope to discuss the special meaning and practice of the religious vows in an active religious community. As a point of clarification, rather than referring to the "active religious life," I have employed throughout this essay the expression "participative religious life," the reasons for which will become clear as the text proceeds.

A prudent thinker does not develop his thoughts in solitude but invites expert fellowmen to discuss how they may be communicated with clarity and refinement. Especially when certain ideas have not to his knowledge been expressed in past or contemporary thought, he feels the need for support and correction. Both have been granted to me abundantly by the executive director of the Institute of Man, Bert van Croonenburg, the assistant director, Susan Annette Muto, and by Sister Mary Aquinas Healy, contributor to the publications of the Institute. Without their excellent suggestions, which at times amounted to a true participation in this creative effort, this writing would not appear as it does now. However, they should not be held responsible for these ideas nor for their final mode of expression.

The Questioning of Religious Life

PERSONALITY FULFILLMENT IN THE SPIRITUAL LIFE, the first book in this series, brought new insight to the meaning of the life of the spirit as a life of presence inspired by the sacredness of people, things and events in their deepest reality. In that book, coming to a basic understanding of what the spiritual life means to mankind in general was of central importance, while in the present volume, one particular way of living this life — the religious — will be our main concern.

It cannot be overemphasized that today people in all areas of life — from government to factory — are questioning the foundation and meaning of even the most sacred customs and institutions. The religious life falls prey to this insecurity not only on the outside but within the confines of the religious community itself. The religious can look upon this insecurity more as a challenge than as a source of disruption and dismay, provided he can first look to himself and ask what personal attitude is at the root of his questioning.

Negative Moods

A question is already prejudiced by the mood out of which it grows. If I start out in a negative frame of mind, I may end with an answer that is destructive and harmful instead of constructive and illuminating. For example, if I ask my question under the influence of resentment about slights which I may have endured, my most likely response will be bitter, representing a one-sided, negative viewpoint only. Let me reflect, then, on the sources of the negative moods in which I may question the religious life.

The first mood is that of disappointment. It should not be surprising that I experience misunderstanding, envy, and jealousy in my community. By necessity, it is a human community filled with sinners, not saints. It is at once a paradise of splendid intentions and a jungle of egoistic desires, anxieties, and passions that permeate every human group in need of redemption.

Another source of the negative mood may be a defensive attitude toward my own failure. Personally I may have fallen away from my original commitment to my vocation. Deep within me I am upset by a sense of failure, guilt, and humiliation. I cannot live with constant reproach. Therefore, I try to repress my feelings by developing defensive theories and stories to prove that the community to which I belong, not I, is blameworthy. It is easy to be victimized by this defense. Community life, like all human life, is filled with certain ugly, evil and demonic incidents that mark any human togetherness.

A third possibility is that I may have become exasperated by the lack of vision and refinement, the mediocrity, inanity, puerility, or dull-wittedness of certain religious around me. Again we must remember that communities draw their members from a contemporary society. The standards of this culture may be so mediocre and pragmatic that those drawn from it may not be able to rise above a vulgar "regular guy" attitude in spite of having memorized textbooks in philosophy and theology. Disgusted by the paucity of creative men and women of vision and refinement, I may again be inclined to question religious life in the wrong mood. What I question is not this life as such but the local traditions which limit it and may temporarily halt its progress.

Moreover, questioning religious life is frequently a participation in the interrogation of others who write about it in newspapers, periodicals, and books. These authors, too, write in certain moods which may be negative, resentful, or defensive, especially when they themselves may have failed to live up to the ideal, or may have suffered deeply from the repulsive, nasty attitudes one is bound to encounter in some superiors or fellow religious. The mood of an essay is often more influential than its factual content. What is said may be less pernicious for my peace of mind than the manner in which it is communicated. The resentful or negative mood of a one-sided publication may color my mood and tarnish my vision. Under such influence, I may become sensitive to only the coarse side of life in the community, confusing its temporal and local inadequacies with its eternal meaning and foundation. Hence, before questioning my religious life and its meaning, it is wise to define the mood which prompts my question in the first place.

Conditions for Proper Questioning

I can set out on my search for the true meaning of religious life in a positive, enriching way on the condition that I approach it with a sense of mystery. The emergence of religious life in Christianity is a mystery of grace that will never be completely understood or unveiled by human intelligence. This mystery of grace is compounded by the dark mystery of iniquity in me and my neighbors, which is always as ready to prostitute the gift of grace as it is to confound the gift of religious life. The repeated deterioration of goodness in men of all ages is as difficult to comprehend as the fact that my own inclination for evil can exist alongside my own call to grace. Therefore, developing a sense of the mystery of grace is essential if I am to encounter fully the divine gift of religious life. Grounded in this sense, my questions will be prayerful questions. I shall not try aggressively to wrest the answer from God or man because I shall be deeply aware that every answer is a gift and every insight a grace. The agitation and willfulness of the resentful or compulsive religious will not plague me. I will feel in harmony with the great questioners of the religious life, with Teresa of Avila, Libermann, Saint Bernard, and John of the Cross.

I should also distinguish between central questions about religious life and peripheral ones. The former concern its deepest meaning and foundation, its very existence, while the latter are directed to certain customs, to temporal style or local adaptation. As soon as I become engrossed in peripheral questions, making no attempt to link them to the central ones, I lose my perspective and direction, perhaps even making the fatal mistake of dealing with a peripheral question as if it were central. So doing, I affirm or condemn the mystery of religious life on the basis of its accidental, temporary appearances. In contrast, the man who attempts to answer the central questions first can deal with the peripheral ones later without losing his way.

Why, I may ask, should I be concerned with peripheral questions at all, once I have answered the central ones? Peripheral problems deal with the concrete incarnation of the ideals of religious life within my culture and life situation, and peripheral questioning is essential if this incarnation is to be actualized in daily practice. Its absence would mean the death of dynamism in convent and monastery. The participation of religious communities in the history of humanization is the basis of the necessity to question repeatedly the concrete structure of this life within the cultures in which it emerges. However, such questioning should never take place in total separation from central or foundational questioning.

Finally, in questioning religious life I must be humbly aware of my own limitations. Immoderate questioning destroys me. I can bear only a limited burden of doubt. I can go only so far without losing balance, equanimity and wholeness. When I pass these limits I feel tense, depressed and anxious; I experience diffusion, tiredness and disgust. This response is the warning sign that I should temporarily abstain from questioning until I have regained the composure which allows me to resume in a serene and peaceful mood.

When I am once again peacefully present to the

question, my existence empties itself of its egocentric preoccupations and I am open for the revelation of the reality of religious life in its sacred dimensions. My readiness for such a revelation is based partly on the conviction that questioning any object, event or situation can elicit a spiritual response. Of course, some situations evoke this response more easily than others. Nonetheless, any human encounter, task or study may become a beautiful entrance into the divine if I am ready to discover its presence.

Responsive Presence

My mode of response is determined not only by the uniqueness of the life situation which comes to meet me but also by the uniqueness of my own personality. My presence must be in tune with my individuality; I cannot literally imitate the prayers, attitudes and feelings of a person who differs from me. I have to discover my unique mode of religious life in the course of my existence. And I cannot find this mode simply by logical reasoning. Logical reasoning is an activity of my secluded, isolated intelligence. I need experiential reasoning. Experiential reasoning does not exclude logical thinking but keeps this logic constantly in tune with experienced and lived reality. In day-to-day life I should not be daydreaming, abstract and superficial but truly alive in the place where I am. If I am not present here and now, if I am dwelling in the past, or anxiously anticipating the future, or absorbed in egocentric and false ambitions, I can neither hear God's voice nor understand how this voice speaks silently to me.

At the moment of grace, however, my vision is clear, my perception is acute. I am open for all possible revelations of the meaning of religious life. On the other hand, my inordinate self-preoccupation with my career or my holiness makes it impossible for me to sense the presence of God and the response He asks. The noise of my self-centeredness dims the clarity of His voice. I may not be able to live the fullness of this responsive presence to my vocation at every moment, but through God's gift I may be able to be thus present repeatedly in the many pauses of my daily life. The radiance of these pauses will permeate the other moments in which my religious life may be less full but still real, sustained as it is by the moment of full presence. If I, with God's grace, may grow after many years to such a life, then I shall finally fulfill, in and with Him, what I truly am. Then every day can be only a good day; every season, a good season.

The condition of sensing God in the religious life lies not in the sharpening of my senses but in a specific fundamental mode of life which pervades my whole personality. This fundamental mode of presence implies a self-forgetting attentiveness, a profound relaxed concentration on the situation here and now, a merging of myself with my situation and the people whom I encounter in such a way that I discover in them God Himself. This mode of presence is in fact already mine if only my self-preoccupied ego, cleansed from distracting thought and unclouded by anxious questioning, allows me humbly to accept my life as it is, in the light of the Divine Presence, without fixing myself on any limited aspect of my situation. To be fully present, I must let go; I must allow the stream of self-centered thoughts and feelings to evaporate into the nothingness of my nonattention. When I reach this void of self-centered thoughts and feelings, then I may be fully present to the deepest meaning of religious life. It is this mood which should guide my questioning of the religious life.

Worship and Culture

Worship is the wellspring of culture and the source of my participation in the unfolding of humanity. The meaning of worship in life and culture may be illuminated by the sense of reverence which, though not yet worship, is its spontaneous beginning. Reverence may overwhelm me when I look quietly at the stars, climb a mountain, walk along the ocean's shore, or dwell in the silence of forest and desert. I feel small in the perspective of such beauty and majesty, but somehow I do not feel alienated, forlorn, or threatened. I feel carried by the vast expansion of nature transcending me in space and time. My life becomes a passing moment in the immense and continuous whole which extends itself indefinitely. Humbly acknowledging my position, I experience reverence.

Reverence is the flower of humanization. Its source is the sacred fascination I experience in the presence of the transcendent. Everything worthy of my deepest dedication receives meaning from its relatedness to that mystery which overwhelms me in moments of silent contemplation. Outside this mystery, each appearance of reality loses its radiance and fails to evoke my reverence. Reverence is neither instinct nor custom. Facing the unknown, I may feel instinctive fear. But I must refine this fear into awe by loving acceptance of a higher reality which embraces me as a mystery of love and generosity. Reverence is fear become awe under the mitigating and sublimating influence of loving surrender to a mystery which attracts me by its goodness while keeping me at humble distance by its majesty. The more I grow in reverence, the more it permeates my thought, feeling, movement, and appearance. Ultimately, respect and reverence at the root of my being grant each one of my acts its deepest human meaning.

Awe leads to worship and adoration when I open myself to the ground of this mysterious universe. This experience may engulf me when I discover myself as a source of my own activity and feel, at the same time, that even as personal source I am emerging from the mystery that transcends me. I realize that something higher than I must be the source of personal, cosmic, and cultural unfolding. My limitations in space, time, and possibilities reveal to me that there must be a ground of unfolding infinitely more source and infinitely more person than I am. I experience the Holy in and beyond me as the transcosmic and transpersonal source of my own being, thought, and creation. I feel holy fear of this divine source from which my personal being flows, and still I am attracted by this effusive love which allows me to be and become. Awe permeates me. Before Him I feel as nothing. His mystery is overwhelming, fascinating, and fear-evoking. I could not face it if I did not experience also that He is the highest Good and the origin of all goodness in myself, mankind, and world. Worship is saying yes to this dependency, enjoying that I am nothing, that He is all. This is adoration, highest expression of reverence and respect.

Respect, not fear, is the root of culture and humanization. I freely maintain respect for that which I experience as higher than I am. The spontaneous response which flows from reverence is free, flexible, and creative, and therefore a source of living culture. Fear which stems from man's perception of threatening power may lead to reactions which are unfree and fixated. These reactions hamper the unfolding of culture, stifle initiative, and frustrate leisure and playfulness at the heart of my cultural presence. I cannot deny that respect, though not yet deepened to worship, is already a trustworthy ground of culture. However, this is so only as long as my respect does not close itself off from its own possibility to become worship and to root itself in presence to the Holy.

When I refuse to keep myself reverently open for this possibility, I may make one or the other isolated appearance of nature or culture my ultimate ground or purpose, thereby hindering the objective unfolding of the culture as a whole. Respect isolated from worship may develop into idolatry. For example, I may make the ultimate and exclusive aim of life my family, profession, country, or some vested interest of the class or group to which I belong. Idolizing one value in the culture may lead me to betray my fundamental faithfulness to other demands of the unfolding of mankind and world. When my cultural respect, on the other hand, is rooted in worship of the One Who transcends culture, inspires its unfolding, and grants every value its proper place, I am open to the demands of objective unfolding in each of my cultural acts and creations. Loss of worship in a culture weakens respect and thereby culture itself. The disappearance of respect resulting from the death of worship may lead to the return of unsublimated fear as the only means to maintain order, for worship fosters cultural respect and is a safeguard of its unfolding.

The deepest ground of culture can thus be found in man's attitude of reverence, respect and worship. This perception implies that each cultural act carries more than the mere functional meaning of effecting an observable change. Also present is a deeper meaning which transcends the immediately visible change. My presence in worship becomes a reverent listening to reality in its deepest meaning, manifested in a respectful love for others and a respectful presence to things. I tend beyond the veil of appearances to penetrate the mystery of the Holy as it appears in every manifestation of reality. I see the other person or object emerging in the splendor of uniqueness out of the ground of the sacred. The immediate and the transcendent dimensions of what I encounter are by no means mutually exclusive. On the contrary, the transcendent reveals itself in the immediate and the immediate reveals itself as potentially transcendent. To be fully human I should grow in the ability to discover the sacred dimension of all that is, in spite of the fact that I can be overwhelmed and blinded by immediate appearances and their demands on my affections, time and energy.

Thus far I have considered only the most fundamental meaning expressed in my cultural acts, which is reverence and worship. The more my acts become personal, the more I am able to express in and through them a commitment to various horizons of meaning. Other possible meanings are, for example, those which express social or aesthetic values. Without being exhaustive I may enumerate as an example, a set of values usually present in the behavior of eating which has reached, in a balanced way, the fullness of cultural meaning. I shall ascend from lower, more restricted meanings to higher, more comprehensive ones. The higher values will not eliminate the lower ones but rather penetrate and elevate them.

A first meaning of eating is fulfillment of the needs which this special kind of behavior by its very nature tends to fulfill. Eating should naturally fulfill my need for nourishment. The meaning of my meal as nourishment should not be negated but elevated by the higher social and aesthetic values which are expressed in the manner in which I eat. I should lack cultural balance if I allowed table ceremonies and manners to dominate to such a degree that I should leave the table dignified but hungry.

The first value which transcends simple need fulfillment is that of self-actualization. As a cultured man, I consume the kind and amount of food compatible with the actualization of my higher self. At times I may even abstain from food so that I may serve the actualization of the spirit. Another meaning of my cultural endeavor is to foster the unfolding of mankind and world. As a human being, I do not live, grow, and act in isolation; I should always be concerned about my fellowman. The practice of refined table manners benefits not only me and the man opposite me, but also all mankind insofar as a dehumanizing way of eating diminishes the humanizing forces in the world and weakens the valuable codes in which humanity has expressed these forces. The same may be said of the aesthetic value of eating as it is incarnated and promoted by cultured behavior. Mankind has developed countless ways of preparing meals aesthetically in style and arrangement of table settings and in the serving of courses. I may express yet another attitude and value in the blessing of my meal and in the grace which I say afterward. Thus, I manifest my dependency on the Most High by dedicating my meal to Him Who is the source of my being. Only now do I arrive at the highest possibility of my cultural act, that of worship. Thus, the values embodied in the act of nourishment imply a progression from lower to higher. Culture is humanizing and sanctifying when it opens each cultural participant to the possibility of expressing values and meanings in their proper hierarchy.

The process of humanization would be a smooth and uninterrupted development if it were not steadily disrupted by factors which halt, and may even reverse and distort, this upward movement of cultivation. Two main destructive forces are the functional specialization and the innate egoism of man.

Function and Culture

In the beginning of his history, man did not face the conflict between functional specialization and the deepest foundation of culture. Harvesting, seeding, hunting and dancing naturally embodied his openness to the realm of worship. He experienced these activities as interwoven with the survival of his tribe, the care of his family, and the worship of his gods. He expressed his aesthetic presence in dancing, in the carving on his tools, and in the designs on the walls of his cave. Long before the functional and technical era, man's openness to fundamental human values and their embodiment in his cultural acts and creations was facilitated by a certain inner unification of life.

Contemporary man has progressed greatly in his functional, technical and scientific development. The resulting body of skill and knowledge makes it possible for us to expand more effectively than ever the human values which we are called to unfold. However, increasing functional specialization may blind me to the human values which should sustain and guide my life. The functional may preoccupy me to the point of negating my presence to those values which constitute the very soul of culture. Higher values are threatened by the poison of mere functionality as well as by those values which are lower on the scale but still essential. For example, a scientist or businessman may be so enamored of the prospect of increasing perfection in laboratory or sales techniques that he does not take into account his bodily needs which demand sufficient nourishment, relaxation, and recreation. Functional value may dominate at the expense of the value of need fulfillment. Or the same person may become so involved in practical endeavors that he neglects his family. Here again is a perversion of the fullness of the cultural act by the functional. The actualization of his family and the fulfillment of its needs should inspire, guide, and motivate his functional endeavors. The same observation may be made of other realms of cultural meaning, such as the social, aesthetic, and religious. The higher, and therefore more fundamental, the value in which my cultural act is rooted, the more liable it is to be negated by the functional attitude.

Distortion of Culture by Egocentrism

Another threat to objective cultural unfolding is my inclination to distort the true hierarchy of values which should be embodied in my acts if I wish them to be well-balanced. This propensity is rooted in my innate egoism. As we have already seen, a well-balanced cultural act expresses various human values simultaneously. Some of these, the religious and social for example, are higher than others, such as the fulfillment of individual bodily needs. I should clearly distort the cultural balance of my life if I were to make the fulfillment of my own bodily needs so central that I should neglect to take into account my religious obligations or tread unjustly upon the rights of others. On my value scale, each higher value should prevail over the lower and determine the limits of its influence on my behavior.

The most fundamental value is the transcendent meaning of every one of my acts. This is true not only for my personal activities but for the enterprises of groups of people and of the culture as a whole. The transcendent value should always prevail; this alone can guarantee the full unfolding of the culture. Vested self-centered interests of groups and individuals are lower on the scale of values to be incarnated in cultural endeavors than, for example, religious, social, and humanist values. Cultural ventures distorted by an exclusive domination of vested interests delay and distort the true unfolding of humanity. I should thus be concerned not only with the threat of mere functional involvement but also with that of the innate self-centeredness of man and society which may close off their openness to higher values.

For example, a man may be so involved in the interests of his family that he would readily sacrifice any higher value if this would imply his promotion of the welfare of those dear to him. Or a person may be linked so intimately with a business or a school system that he would refuse the demands of necessary cultural development if they were to harm the vested interests of his organization. Another person may be so involved with the lower values of status, popularity, and material possessions that he would betray the true unfolding of the culture if this were to mean loss of status, decrease in salary, and diminution of popularity as expressed in the confidence and approval of others. Egocentrism may even extend itself to a person's attitude toward the whole of humanity. In this case, the service of man becomes the ultimate value and godless humanism the criterion of culture, in spite of the fact that many forms of humanism do imply a mystique manifesting a type of religious concern. Another form of human self-centeredness is that of scientism. Here scientific knowledge becomes the final aim and guide of cultural development.

We may conclude that it is openness and unconditional commitment to the transcendent meaning of the culture which ultimately enable man to transcend egoism in himself and society and to remain faithful to the objective unfolding of mankind and the world.

Culture and Value Radiation

Each man feels called by grace, temperament, ability, personal history and unique inspiration to develop his own profile of life in which one or more basic modes of presence to reality will prevail, while other fundamental modes, though developed less strongly, will not be closed off entirely. The total closure of one or the other fundamental human presence to people and things would lead to a distortion of the human personality. By means of such modes of presence every man remains open, at least implicitly, to every basic cultural value. However, it is difficult for the average man living in our broken civilization to remain open to these values of his own accord. Therefore, persons and institutions witness for particular values by living and promoting them in concentrated, unique ways. In other words, when a culture has lost its initial wholeness and unity and has differentiated into specialties, it becomes desirable, and even necessary, to set some members free to foster, for instance, the aesthetic openness which should be present to some degree in all of us. Less differentiated cultures, which still experience religious, aesthetic and practical dimensions of human life as an original unity lived by all, do not find it necessary to free members as special witnesses and guardians for one or the other value orientation. Since these fundamental modes of presence are lived spontaneously by all, none of them are threatened with forgetfulness, extinction, or neglect.

But once the original wholeness of value experience has been broken under the influence of specialization, it becomes clear that some value orientations will be in danger of extinction.

Whether or not a value orientation will be forgotten or fostered depends partly on the culture. A great culture is one which upholds a variety of cultural institutions and interests. For example, the literary life supports poets, novelists, and teachers of literature, all of whom help to maintain the sensitive poetic dimension of human existence. A culture is outstanding to the degree that it allows as many cultural groups as possible to concentrate on the development of fundamental dimensions of human presence. Each group then represents one dimension of the openness of the population to the whole of reality. Each keeps the population in tune with an important value which might otherwise be lived in a mediocre way or neglected totally.

The process of humanization thus implies that the culture frees certain men and women to concentrate on the development of certain fundamental styles or modes of life. Some may concentrate on poetry; others on ontology, science, or religious presence. All are called to achieve excellence in the one dimension which they are free to foster in a special way. To be sure, an exceptional person may develop a greater excellence in a particular aspect of life than those who are specializing in it as average men and women. But this is accidental. Cultural institutions are necessarily made up of average men and women like you and me and not geniuses. For example, it is the average teacher of literature who fosters the day by day cultural openness to the poetic aspect of life to which the great poet witnesses once in a century. However, the average person will not attain the same outstanding development in this dimension of life as another average person who, *together with others*, is permitted by society to concentrate on the growth of his specific interest.

We may conclude that a predominantly functional society remains value-conscious by the emergence in its midst of centers of value-presence. Today our culture allows many of its members to specialize their lives in a specific presence to certain values which might otherwise be forgotten in the functioning of society. For example, we find specialists who represent the value of bodily need fulfillment. Such persons as doctors, nurses, masseurs, and athletic trainers keep man open to an awareness of his bodily needs, needs he might easily neglect under the pressure of functional involvement. Similarly, people are set free for psychological or aesthetic values, respectively as social workers, psychotherapists, and counselors, or as poets, painters, designers, and teachers of art appreciation. The same may be said concerning the religious value. I myself, as a participative religious, have been set free to witness for the sacred dimension of all cultural endeavors.

We have seen that the whole of contemporary culture is permeated by strong forces of functional involvement. Within this functional field, however, concentrated centers of people are set free by society to witness for nonfunctional values. Their involvement in these values radiates toward those of us who are preoccupied with other areas of life. Somehow their radiation of concentrated openness for particular values awakens in us our own dormant openness for these values.

I can imagine this value radiation as a wave-like movement in my culture. The wave starts from the concentrated core of a specific value presence in the culture; initially it affects those people who are most open to the particular value. They form quite naturally a cluster of value radiation around the core. Their interest and commitment engenders a second wave insofar as they radiate the same value openness to others around them, who in turn influence those in their own circle toward concern for the value. In this way, a wave-like movement of value awareness is fostered among the population at large. To illustrate, we may consider the aesthetic value. The core of people committed to aesthetic awareness is formed by poets and painters, by professional teachers of art and literature, curators of museums, and patrons of the arts. The cluster is formed by those people who cannot be completely free for this life of artistic openness, but who form the receptive audience around the core. They promote aesthetic interest in daily life by communicating to others what they experience in dialogue with those who are free to devote their lives to the aesthetic. The communication of this cluster in turn arouses others among their families, business and professional associates, and circles of friends to become more acutely aware of the aesthetic dimension of life.

Similarly, some persons, like myself, have been set free by society to dedicate their lives primarily to an openness for the religious dimension of the culture. Around our core forms a cluster of others intensely interested in worship of the Holy and in witness for this most fundamental value. In dialogue with those at the core, they grow increasingly in religious openness which they communicate in turn to others.

Radiation of the Religious Value

As a participative religious, I witness for worship together with others who are equally set free by society to dedicate their lives to an openness for the religious dimension of life and culture. We form a community of average persons freed from the manifold involvements implied in the care of a family. I make myself free for this value radiation by abdicating the founding of a family, and therewith the intense personal concerns, emotional problems, practical distractions, and functional occupations that necessarily accompany family responsibility. The religious community should not be so absorbing functionally and emotionally as the community of marriage tends to be. My vow of celibacy means that I freely sacrifice my right to found a family of my own precisely because I realize that my consequent practical involvement would interfere with the unique style and intensity of worshipping and witnessing which I feel called to live.

The family is a most intricate and demanding unit of care. In order to foster and develop a complex group of dependent, vulnerable, not yet productive children, parents must involve themselves generously in innumerable detailed activities necessary for the protection and growth of each member. As every psychotherapist or marriage counselor can testify, it is often difficult to keep open one's awareness of the transcendent meaning of the other when besieged by the myriad preoccupations characteristic of a small family unit fighting for survival and expansion in a demanding society. The fact that a society has reached a high peak of culture and welfare does not diminish, and perhaps even increases, this preoccupation because the family unit in an advanced culture must see to it that each member participates in the culture. For example, the college education typical of more developed cultures leads to an increase of work and responsibility on the part of parents to ensure that their children will be able to enter college at the right time, with the right preparation, and with sufficient economic sustenance.

The transcendent meaning of people and things can easily be overlooked by a society in which daily cares and special demands are increasingly overwhelming. And yet if the transcendent meaning is lost, life loses what makes it basically worth living. In spite of the onslaught of functional and emotional problems which relate to the immediate appearances of people and things, humanity is still called to keep open both immediate and transcendent dimensions. Now, if the intensive functional and emotional care necessary to maintain a family tends to foster preoccupation with the immediate and interferes with openness for the transcendent, it is not so surprising that the contrasting state of religious celibacy has come to symbolize the aspect of openness for transcendence. Celibacy in the wider sense means keeping oneself free for the appearance of the transcendent, or to put it differently, guarding against being overwhelmed by the functional and emotional aspects of life. This is not to say that married love or married life does not have its own celibate component; it does in the repeated moments of transcendence of the aspects of functional care. Indeed, the immediate appearance of the other is often pervaded by a presence to his or her transcendent meaning. But one cannot deny that such transcendence is at times difficult in married life. Thus it is especially appropriate today for communities of people to gather together in a special way to witness for the transcendent openness so necessary to man's growth as man. As we have seen, every man is called to the fullness of culture; he is called to live a life of religious presence. Married or single, involved in religious endeavors or secular enterprises, man is intended to be a presence to the Holy in all that he is and achieves.

Man humanizes himself to the degree that he is obediently open to unfolding reality, develops respectful love for his fellowman, and reverently lives with and enjoys the situations which life reveals to him. Moreover, man as incarnated spirit experiences in this respectful openness an attraction to the immediate appearances of people and things and at the same time an attraction to their transcendent ground, their rootedness in the Holy. To prevent his presence to immediate appearances from overwhelming his transcendent presence, man must foster a transcendent or celibate element in his life. To do so, humanity needs special groups of witnesses. It is, therefore, quite natural that in cultures, both east and west, groups of men and women emerged to witness for the transcendent or celibate aspect of man's fundamental presence to the immediate manifestations of reality.

How a specific religious community perceives the relationship between the transcendent and the immediate is dependent on the religious view of the culture from which it emerges. For example, religious life fostered by Eastern religions tends almost to dismiss the truth and value of immediate appearances, preferring to concentrate on contemplative presence to the transcendent. Christian religious life, on the other hand, is based on the doctrine of incarnation, which implies a profound respect for immediate appearances as embodiments of the Holy. Therefore, all Christian religious life, even the most contemplative, is involved somewhat in immediacy. It ordinarily abstains, however, from that type of involvement which, according to the accumulated experience of mankind, makes it more difficult for the average person to witness the highest possible intensity of presence to the transcendent meaning of people, situations and events. The daily care of a family may become part of man's path to holiness, but it may also render more difficult his keeping open to the transcendent dimension of life. Some persons have been called to point the way to transcendence by representing for mankind the full development of this necessary dimension of life and by abstaining to some degree from other types of involvement. Hence, religious abstain from the intense daily care of a family and the subsequent personal concern for the collection and maintenance of private possessions.

The basis of all religious life is the intensity and exclusiveness of presence to the Holy. Not all religious live this presence in the same way, and here we discover the foundation for the distinction between the contemplative and the participative religious. The goal of contemplative life is presence to the Holy as revealing itself in the solitude of monastic existence, while the goal of participative religious life is presence to the Holy as revealing itself in the unfolding of the culture. The contemplative religious witnesses for worship in solitude and recollection, while the participative religious witnesses for worship of the Holy in his very act of participation in the culture. For this reason, contemplative religious abstain from certain tasks, studies and social actions which are highly valued in participative religious life. Predominantly contemplative groups serve participative communities by reminding them that their presence to the Holy within these tasks and studies can easily be endangered by preoccupation with the immediate values of the enterprises concerned. Without the example of contemplatives, religious groups who witness for the presence to the Holy in a manner more participative, though not marital or privately economic, may lose themselves totally in their immediate involvements and thus lose their very meaning as religious communities.

Thus, the full unfolding of religious presence in a culture presupposes a hierarchy of religious communities alike in a basic abstinence from the more absorbing human involvements, such as functional and emotional family care, but different in the degree and kind of withdrawal from other less absorbing human engagements. The purpose of their abstinence, like that of the poet from business or the scholar from intensive social life, is not a condemnation of these involvements but a realistic admission that it is impossible to be intensely involved in disparate styles of life and at the same time be a special witness for one style which, in this particular case, uniquely manifests the transcendent presence to the Holy in us all.

Religious Life and Culture

It may now be clear that the participative religious life may guarantee not only religious openness within a civilization but also the true cultural unfolding of mankind. This assumption presupposes, of course, that the religious life is lived in the right way. If this condition is fulfilled, then the greatest blessing for any civilization is the all-permeating presence of participative religious who constantly purify the true cultural unfolding of mankind by silently exposing egocentric and group-centered interests through a fundamental presence to the transcendent meaning of the culture.

This religious presence has more the nature of receptivity than of aggressive activity. Presence to the Holy is a gift, not a conquest. The more I am open to the gift of worship, the more my cultural activities will seem to share the luminous quality of Light. My deeds will be the expression of my increasing spirituality, while my presence to the sacred meaning of the culture will become increasingly natural and gracious. My own cultural participation may enable others to witness my life of presence to the sacred meaning of the culture and to respond to its development, style and expression. As a religious, I may appear to live somehow apart from the busy world of practical involvement. It is as if I see the culture in which I participate in a way my fellowman does not see, as if my cultural activity is guided by motives other than his. Sometimes he feels so because he perceives only the surface of the cultural activities and purposes we share. He may not yet fully understand the meaning which penetrates their depth. His many immediate preoccupations, his unconscious needs for popularity, power, and possessions, reinforced by the standards of the everyday world, incline him to live on a level of existence which does not touch the deepest meaning of his daily life.

This response to my life is not strange, for my religious presence, structured by the revelation of Christianity, inspired and supported by Grace, is supernatural and supercultural, and may be therefore initially alien to my cultural participant. Yet as a religious I may surprise him with the gracious ease and naturalness with which I am present to my task. It may be difficult for him to understand why I am less preoccupied with status and success. Especially when these have become the primary meaning of his task, he may question my motivations. He may even suspect ulterior motives, such as an increase of worldly influence for my church or community. As long as his perception is limited by the superficial dimensions of his cultural task and his immediate needs, it will be impossible for him to make sense out of my life. He may even think that I suffer from some psychological quirk when he sees how dedicated I am to the fostering of our common cultural task without much concern for material gain or ego-enhancement. When he is gradually compelled to admit that I am personally stable, serene, and well-integrated, one explanation still open to him may be to perceive my wholehearted involvement as inspired by group egoism. However, when he discovers that my activity is not aimed primarily at convert-making or at enhancing the status, reputation and richness of my church or religious community, then he may no longer be able to escape the insight that my cultural involvement is a mystery. This experience may evoke his curiosity. Grace may play on his curiosity, evoking in him the suspicion that there *is* another unseen dimension to the cultural task which, though it eludes him, must be the explanation of my passionate and yet serene engagement in manual labor, science or art.

Gradually grace may unveil to him his own possibility for openness to the transcendent value of every cultural endeavor. Once this happens to him, he will experience to his surprise that his cultural task does not fade into a mere illusion; instead, it radiates throughout all of its aspects the grace and substance which it has lacked up to this moment of his life. The hidden value of all culture is magnificently revealed to him. He transcends the dual order of immediate and transcendent presence, combining both in a unity of experience and action. Such unification is not a performance of his logical intelligence but a transcendent experience which embraces his whole being. He may discover that the various modes of participation in the culture are not isolated modes of living which must be integrated laboriously into a unified personality; rather, his presence to the Holy is the single center of energy from which emerge modes of cultural participation which manifest and radiate the religious presence which he is at the core of his personality.

As a good religious participant, I should be deeply sensitive and deeply spiritual at the same time; sensitive to the immediate aspects of my cultural companions and tasks, and spiritual insofar as my cultural participation is an act of worship originating in the initiative which flows from my presence to the Holy. My way of life should transform the appearance of the most transient and apparently insignificant events into a meaningful, radiant, and eternal value. When I am present to daily events as revelations of the Holy, they are at once what they are and something other than they seem to be. When my presence to the Holy lights up daily reality, I perceive eternal values present even in the most insignificant appearances. To live in worship is to pass beyond visible reality and attain the unseen truth in daily events. This experience occurs when I animate the humblest of acts with the light of the spirit.

When God gives me the grace to be present to the sacred meaning of daily reality, I may be an invitation to others to rediscover the spiritual in the cultural. My very mode of presence may reveal to them the source from which all men are called to draw meaning in life. I do not offer myself as a "shining example" to my cultural participants, but I invite each person to find within himself the model to which he must conform. I am merely a help insofar as I may remind him, more by my life than by my words, that he should be present to the Holy in a manner of worship which brings out his own uniqueness. Worshipping the Holy in and through my cultural participation, I may evoke a similar attitude in my cultural companion. But I can never force his awareness. Indeed, it may well be that I shall not find in him an openness for worship. If this happens, I should not feel that my life is meaningless or that my task is incomplete. The deepest meaning of my life as a religious participant, the source of its vitality and joy, is my awareness that I as a unique person am answering my call to worship and witness the Holy in and through my cultural task. My fulfillment of this task is a liturgy. Each thought, gesture, and activity is a gracious adoration of the Lord Who makes culture be by maintaining and unfolding man as guardian and creator of His culture in the cosmos. I feel myself cooperating with the Holy; I feel gratefully lifted up in the flow of the sacred history of mankind. I even feel playful before the face of the Most High who daily renews the earth in and through man's cultural endeavors.

There are periods in history in which people are closed to the message of the Holy. God is not dead for them; they are dead for God. It may be that during such periods cultural-religious participants are unable to awaken the dormant possibilities for worship in their fellowmen. This does not mean that the religious participant is useless. On the contrary, he is more needed than ever. For it is precisely during such times that men need the few persons among them — laymen and religious — who will stand in worship before the face of the Holy and consecrate to Him a culture that tries to forget Him. Indeed, such persons are most necessary, for it is quite possible that God spares a culture because of the few who continue to consecrate it to Him in spite of the forgetfulness of others.

This situation may be compared to man's openness for the poetic dimension of life. There are times when the majority of people, because of their practical and economic involvement, become insensitive to their own possibilities for poetic presence. This does not mean that poets are superfluous for mankind in such periods. On the contrary, if there were no poets left as lonely guardians of the poetic dimension of human existence, it would be far more difficult for humanity to find its way back to its own poetic dimension when it awakens again to this deeply human need. The absence of poets and poetry for long periods of time would also mean the loss of concrete styles and modes of poetry which would help a reawakened humanity to respond once more to its poetic dimension. It is true that the lonely poet does not enjoy the eager reception of an adoring and delighted public, but neither is he robbed of the possibility of joy. For the time being, he may find an even deeper joy in poetry itself, in the celebration of language, in his humble presence to all that is revealed to the man who dedicates his life to beauty.

As a religious participant, I am sorely needed by a culture that temporarily forgets the Holy. I have been called to guard man's openness to religious value. When men are once again ready to foster this openness, then they will find to their delight that the religious value, temporarily neglected, has not disappeared, nor has the way of being open to this value been totally closed. But if I make the mistake during these times of rooting the meaning and joy of my life in the effectiveness of the witnessing aspect of my worship, I shall most likely experience disillusion, perhaps even despair. Now and always I should root myself, and the meaning and joy of my project of life, in the delight of celebrating the religious dimension of the culture, of growing daily in the worship of Him who makes all culture be and Whom I encounter intimately in the sacrament of my cultural task.

3

Origin and Originality of the Participative Religious Life

My religious life should be understood in the light of the community to which I belong. Most communities are either contemplative or participative. In this book we are concerned with the participative religious life, though this concern is meant in no way to depreciate the splendor and continuing necessity of the life of contemplation. Today, however, under the impact of history, the participative religious community is coming into its own for the first time. Therefore, the need to clarify the unique meaning of this life is urgent.

Orientation of Contemplative and Participative Religious Life

The participative life is one of religious involvement in the culture, while the contemplative life is primarily one of contemplation. Therefore, the contemplative religious withdraws as far as possible from cultural involvement. Monks and cloistered nuns who spend some part of their time in cultural activities perceive these as a necessary diversion in their concentrated life of worship. Cultural work is for them a means toward contemplation and the maintenance of its conditions; it is not meant to interfere with the readiness of the monk for concentrated presence to God in solitude. Accordingly, rules, customs and spiritual exhortations of contemplative communities tend to stress that no monk should participate in cultural enterprises to such a degree that this involvement would diminish the primacy and totality of his life of contemplation.

Within the contemplative life-orientation the desire to involve oneself wholeheartedly in cultural enterprises would rightly be experienced as a temptation. Thus, many monasteries have preferred menial activities to scientific and artistic endeavors. They have felt that the latter might make it more difficult for the monk to return to the fullness of religious contemplation. Monasteries or monks who have become involved in art and study, on the other hand, have found in the spiritual writings of the great exemplars of monastic life modes of transcending these interests so that they might keep their minds and hearts ready, first of all, for a renewed presence to God in solitude.

The structures of the contemplative community — rules, customs, style of encounter, and even buildings — have been inspired by concern to effect a readiness for contemplation surpassing that found in the active cultural trends shaping human history outside the convent walls.

This orientation differs from the fundamental mode of the participative religious life. The participative religious aims ultimately at a presence to the Holy, revealing and unfolding itself in the very cultural trends in which the contemplative religious must avoid intense involvement in order to remain available for the life of pure contemplation. The contemplative engages in the culture at the sidelines, as it were, in order to be able to be present again to God who reveals Himself in the deepest human solitude. The participative religious, on the other hand, commits himself to hours of prayer, silence, and contemplation in order to be more fully present to the Holy as manifesting Himself in the culture in which he must participate if he hopes to be an effective witness in his chosen mode of religious life. Failure of life marks the contemplative who attempts to escape contemplation by enthusiastic involvement in the cultural endeavors of his contemporaries; for the participative religious the opposite attitude spells failure. When he attempts to flee the sometimes onerous entanglements of administration, cultural enterprise, or social work by seeking to live a contemplative life at hours when he should be task-oriented, he fails his obligations. The exhortations of spiritual directors of contemplatives aim at decreasing cultural involvement. The advice given by spiritual directors to the participative religious urges him to overcome any inertia or disinterestedness he may experience as hindering his wholehearted involvement in study, science, art, or other cultural endeavors.

In former ages, the Holy Spirit inspired men and women to witness for presence to the Holy in cloisters and convents where they could concentrate their whole existence on a contemplative dwelling with God. Such witnesses will always be necessary. Mankind needs to behold certain people who symbolize the truth that the highest human act is adoring contemplation. But as time went on, other men and women, inspired by the Paraclete, felt inclined to witness for the supernatural dimension of the very cultural tasks in and through which humanity constantly evolves itself. Participative religious communities thus emerged from the contemplative and are only now finding their unique meaning within the mysterious plan of the Holy. Certain structures of the contemplative community still influence the participative religious life. As a result, this life may be inspired by two seemingly contrary principles: that of being primordially available to total contemplation in solitude and isolation, and that of being primordially available to the inspiration of God as present in the unfolding culture. The participative religious may feel somewhat like an amphibious creature in his desire to be at once fully contemplative and fully participative. Trying to combine both goals, he may end up neither a good contemplative nor a worthwhile cultural participant. As an ambiguous presence to reality, he cannot easily reach personal harmony and integration. Moreover, the people with whom he labors cannot experience him as a wholehearted participant. He seems to be a halfhearted alien whose allegiance to their cause they cannot trust. As a result, they may clamor that religious should *not* be participants in the cultural endeavors of mankind, for they seem to be unable to give themselves effectively to the task at hand.

No one can be blamed for the fact that it has taken centuries, and may take still more time, for the participative religious life to differentiate itself clearly and consistently from the contemplative. The emergence of any cultural institution involves a slow process wherein one specialization emerges out of the other under the impact of the changing needs of mankind. Initially, the religious worship and witness of the contemplative was sufficient to keep man open to the transcendent aspect of his cultural, social, and practical endeavors. The various areas of cultural presence were initially far less distinct from one another. They had not evolved into isolated, complex enterprises threatening to absorb totally the energy and attention of those dedicated to them. The less evolved cultural and social structures of life were more closely allied to the deeply religious orientation permeating society as a whole. The population observed certain devotions and religious ceremonies which enabled them to live in presence to the Holy as manifested in social events, crafts, and customs. Moreover, the numerous convents and monasteries found in the midst of the population were constant reminders of man's call to be open to the transcendent aspect of life and culture.

Today, however, under the impact of specialization, specific witnesses must be called forth from the population to live before the eyes of all a presence to the Holy precisely in and through the various cultural acts and creations. Increasing differentiation and specialization of social, scientific, technical, aesthetic, and administrative tasks, and their orientation toward mastery of the world, have made it far more difficult for the average man to be continually aware of the sacredness of cultural development. Thus, over the centuries, under the inspiration of the Holy Spirit, religious communities have of necessity made men and women free to participate in cultural endeavors without becoming so absorbed in social systems and establishments that they are unable to remain faithful to the inner sacred orientation of these cultural enterprises. They should highlight the sacredness of participation in the culture by their involvement in a myriad range of cultural endeavors according to their own talents and dispositions. In this way, participative religious can increasingly permeate humanity, symbolizing and witnessing for all men the unity of the sacred and the profane, of religion and life, of holiness and culture.

Energetic young men and women may desire to serve the culture in a religious way, but simultaneously they may feel confused by the ambiguous attitude of certain religious whom they encounter in school, hospital, office, or art studio. This attitude arises from the confusion between contemplation and participation, and from the futile attempt to find a compromise between the two, rather than realizing that each life is beautiful and unique in its own way. While participative religious may not experience a desire to return to a life of pure contemplation, they may wrongly decide that they should identify themselves only with those works which seem least likely to interfere with the possibility of religious contemplation, such as catechetical instruction, administration of the sacraments, spreading devotions, or teaching the sacred sciences. This tendency toward identification of the sacred with only certain kinds of work finds support in the unchristian split between the holy and the profane, the sacred and the secular, the soul and the body, which have plagued Christianity since its early inception in a Greco-Roman milieu. Another expression of this split can be found in the suggestion that service in the slums among the poor, catechesis or similar apostolic and missionary work, is more "holy" than other tasks and should be done, therefore, by people who are religious. Administration, science, art, and teaching, on the other hand, are fundamentally not so "holy," and therefore should not be engaged in by religious. Another symptom of the religion-life split is the unconscious tendency to identify with one part of the population. In this expression, to labor among the poor and in the foreign missions is "holy;" to serve the needs of the middle class, of university professors or of the rich, is "unholy." However, a religious who has transcended this age-old split knows that all cultural participation can be holy. Both he and his community should realize that all groups of the population are called by Christ, and that religious should be willing to witness for the possibility of openness to the transcendent in all people, in all kinds of endeavors, and, in fact, in every aspect of the modern world.

Diocesan Priest — Priest-Religious

Participative religious life and the life dedicated to the regular care of the spiritual needs of the Catholic population as organized by a diocese are *not* one and the same. Confusion between the two exists partly because the participative religious life has not yet fully emancipated itself from the contemplative life. Because the regular care for souls is bound up with the direct pastoral endeavors of the Church, it offers itself as a seeming compromise between the imagined "holiness" of contemplation and the "unholiness" of cultural endeavors outside regular pastoral care. The resulting identification of the essence of participative religious life with the essence of the life of pastoral care is one of the greatest obstacles to understanding the full and unique meaning of religious life. This confusion is seen in the ambiguity of the man who does not know what in practice *is* the real difference between the life of a diocesan priest and that of the priest who is a member of a religious order. Such ambiguity may account for the increasing numbers of religious who ask permission to become incardinated in dioceses so that they may engage in parish work for a lifetime. The same ambivalence may account for the difficulty vocational directors experience in trying to explain convincingly to high school boys what the concrete differences are between the vocations of the diocesan priest in his parish and the member of a religious order who may be assisting in the same parish. This confusion can lead also to undignified competition between religious communities and diocesan institutes for pastoral care when the participation of the religious in diocesan endeavors is viewed as the essential and ultimate meaning of his religious life. This harmful ambiguity may even embitter missionary-religious when the time comes for them to turn their parishes over to native diocesan priests in the newly emerging dioceses they have helped to create.

Even if I am a religious who happens at a certain moment of my religious life to be ordained, I should realize that I am first a religious and only secondly a priest. To be sure, the priestly dignity and sacramental power can be considered in many respects higher and more primary than the consecrated religious life which I was already living before the Church granted me the power to say Mass and administer sacraments. But I should reflect on the priesthood not only as a sacred order; I should also consider the way in which its concrete functioning in the Church today is usually structured. In the light of this reflection, I should realize that there is a radical difference between the way in which the religious who is ordained should structure his life and the way in which a diocesan priest should do so. To be a religious is a way of life, while the priesthood as such is not a way of life but an office or ministry.

The diocesan priest is called by the Spirit to bind his life exclusively to the pastoral functioning of a diocesan or mission territory located in a clearly delineated geographical area. He generously inserts himself in an existing juridical, administrative, and pastoral system in which he is called to administer to the pastoral needs of an organized subdivision of the Church. He irrevocably and unconditionally identifies his life with the demands of the diocese or mission concerned. His private life is not made free by a community which sustains him, nor lived in accordance with vows which liberate him from many self-concerns. His life remains his own concern, much like the life of the layman. In a sense, I may say that a diocesan priest is an ordained layman, while a priest-religious is an ordained religious. It is true that the Church ordains only laymen who have gone through a specific and prolonged seminary education and who, at least in the Western Church, have not contracted the obligation to care for a family of their own. But it is not *per se* impossible that the Church might grant the priestly office to many more laymen, even if they have a different type of preparation than the traditional seminary training, and even if a certain number of them have married.

The relative freedom from as many social structures and establishments as possible, a characteristic of religious life, and the adoption of a specific way of life called religious, are not typical of the layman who establishes a family nor of those laymen who have been ordained priests. The diocesan priest has been called primarily to care for the overall spiritual needs and problems of the faithful within the framework of the systematic organization of the diocese or mission to which he has pledged himself for a lifetime. His priesthood means a ministry more than a special way of life nourished by the spirituality of a specific community. The diocesan priest is, as it were, the "general practitioner" in the Church without whom Christianity could not hope to reach the great number of people it does today. His presence in great numbers is absolutely necessary for the maintenance and development of the Church.

It would be foolish, and even sinful, to suggest to a man clearly called to join this dedicated diocesan clergy that he should consider the life of the priest-religious, which is essentially a different calling. If we were to convince such a person that the best way to follow his attraction for regular parish care would be to enter religious life, we should in the end greatly harm the essential value of the religious life itself. For such misled laymen might become disgruntled religious who sooner or later would resent the fact that we deceived them into thinking that religious life was the best way to follow their attraction for regular parish care. A religious who happens to be ordained a priest at a certain time in his life, and a layman who directly joins the priesthood as exercised in his diocese, are each in his own unique way necessary for the mysterious development of the kingdom of God among men. And, in one sense, we can readily understand why the function of the diocesan priest is more fundamental for the regular care of the faithful than that of the religious who may also be a priest. The priesthood of the religious is incidental to his religious life orientation and should be lived in accordance with the freedom essential to this life which he embraced long before his ordination as a priest. For example, a religious who participates in the culture as a scientist, social worker, administrator, artist, or manual laborer, and who is also ordained a priest, should not feel obliged to leave his specific field of witnessing because of his ordained state.

His being a priest adds a specific dimension to his cultural participation. First of all, in a psychologically split society people are falsely inclined to experience the cultural as the apex of profane existence and the priesthood as the summit of the life of the sacred. Therefore, the active participation in the culture of a religious who is also a priest is a most striking sign and symbol of the holiness of cultural orientation as long as his witnessing is not distorted by a primary personal striving for status and possessions.

One of the many meanings of the priesthood is to consecrate the truly good and humane by offering it to the Holy from which all goodness flows. The life of religious participation is a life of worship and of consecration of that in which it participates. The Church, therefore, generously allows many participative religious to be ordained priests, so that in their Holy Mass and priestly lives they may in a special way represent and symbolize the consecration of their special fields of endeavor, and of their cultural participants, to the Father of all Light in and through Christ the Redeemer. The priest is the person who *ex officio* consecrates the world in all its natural and cultural dimensions to God. Each day the priest-religious offers to God in his Holy Mass the specific cultural sector in which he participates. He reminds the Lord of all the cultural participants in his chosen field, and when possible, he unites around the altar persons engaged in his own cultural endeavor. In his homily he may direct them to worship *in* and *through* the *cultural* task he shares with them. In this service of the Word he stresses the unity between the liturgical, sacramental life of the Church and his fellow workers as administrators, scientists, artists, scholars, psychiatrists, pastoral counselors, teachers, or social workers. At other times, he may be called to administer the sacraments to persons in his own field of cultural endeavor.

Finally, there develops at certain times a specific pastoral dimension within the special field of the priest-religious. Of increasing daily importance in contemporary life are the cultural endeavors in which men and women are involved. The religious celibate who participates with them in the same task in openness for its transcendent meaning is more sensitive to the problems his colleagues face in attempting to maintain a similar openness to the sacred dimension of their daily task. These colleagues, striving for a spirituality which makes their life and work meaningful, may feel more confident about discussing their difficulties of cultural-religious integration with a priest who is also their coworker in the same area of life. Moreover, his pastoral concern may inspire him to speak and write about the relationship between religion and this specific task which he lives as sacred. The average married man has less time available for such considerations. Likewise, the average diocesan priest is usually too much involved with serving the general pastoral needs of the population; moreover, he has too little first hand experience with specific cultural areas to develop the insight necessary for the creation of a specific integration between religion and these areas. Concentrating on one specialized group of the population would endanger his availability, moreover, for the rest of the people in his parish.

As a religious who is ordained, I may also participate either temporarily or lastingly in the regular pastoral care of parishes or missions. As a matter of fact, historical development has been such that the needs of the Church have made it desirable for large numbers of religious to assume considerable responsibility for regular diocesan care. While it is true that the religious celibate may be needed in diocesan pastoral care and can find fulfillment in it in a way compatible with his calling to be a religious, it also remains true that the administration of a diocese and its parishes is not the primary and essential task of religious who are ordained priests. It is quite right for priest-religious to take over at times the care of parishes or of whole dioceses, as has happened frequently in underdeveloped countries in which the Church was not yet established and could not yet develop a native diocesan clergy. It is a mistake, however, to expand this emergency situation into the normal situation for ordained religious. On the contrary, we must even dare to say that the aim of priest-religious should be to make themselves superfluous as parish priests and as bishops in the diocese which they have taken over as a consequence of a temporary need. In other words, religious celibates who have assumed responsibility for dioceses or parishes should encourage the formation of an indigenous diocesan clergy which may replace them. When the emergency is over, it may then be time for the members of the religious community to return to worship and witness through the cultural participation to which they were called in the first place and for which they have been set free in a special way.

Similarly, just as the Church allows priest-religious to care for dioceses and parishes in times of emergency which may be protracted over centuries, so it also allows certain members of the diocesan clergy to forego the ministry of the parish and involve themselves in specialized cultural endeavors for which only religious are usually set free. The need for priestly and religious witnesses who have the gift of creativity in highly specialized fields of art and science, and who have the ability to develop a synthesis of these fields with the sacred, will always be present. Because of the scarcity of such creative men, we may indeed speak of a lasting need for their contribution. Therefore, at times the Church generously allows exceptional members of her diocesan clergy to forego the ministry to which they are primarily called and to devote themselves for as long as they are needed to tasks which cannot be sufficiently carried out by religious alone. As in the case of the assignment of priest-religious to pastoral care in dioceses and parishes, I should realize that assignment of diocesan priests to cultural-religious specialization is fundamentally meant to fill a need of the Church — not to indicate what the essential life task of the average diocesan priest should be.

The kingdom of God among men is served by Christians who care for the regular needs of the family in an openness to the Holy, and by unmarried Christians who foster the development of the culture in a holy and transcendent way. In order to assist these Christians in their openness for the Holy, the Church ordains some of them as priests who assume the lifelong obligation to minister to the general pastoral needs of the faithful through organized parishes or other communities of faithful organized in accordance with local and temporal conditions. For example, army chaplains serve the general needs of enlisted men. The Church also allows certain men and women to witness for the sacred by a life of contemplation in presence to the Holy. Others sustain the openness of all mankind for the Holy by a life of cultural religious participation. Theirs is a special witness for the Holy in the cultural endeavors of mankind. By their full participation and presence, they exemplify the unity between culture and religion.

The kingdom of God as a witness of Christians for His presence in the world is thus served by people in many different roles. It is the Church's responsibility to be attentive to specific spiritual needs which may require diocesan priests or priest-religious to be temporarily engaged in activities which do not primarily flow forth from the structure of their life commitment. The Church is highly respectful of the personal vocation of its celibates and seldom imposes alien tasks on men obviously not called to serve in certain roles.

We should also point out the problems which may arise in regard to the part-time participation in regular parish care by a priest-religious who has dedicated his life to a specific scientific, aesthetic, or social task. It may be that I can structure my life as a religious in such a way that over and above my specific cultural-religious task I can participate in a form of organized parish care. But it may also happen that I am inspired by the Holy to involve myself more intensely in a specific cultural area, and therefore I should experience participation in parish activity as interfering with my personal primary mission as a religious in the world of culture and social action. For example, the priest religious who is a painter, writer, composer or artist may experience that such participation distracts him from the steady concentration and recollection necessary for the maintenance of the creative flow and expression of his ideas. The gift of creativity demands conditions which vary from person to person. Some creative priest-religious are able to engage in many outside activities — to socialize, meet people, aid in pastoral counseling — without suffering any interruption of their creative powers. Others have to distance themselves from pastoral and social life in order to concentrate on their primary field. After the interruption of pastoral duties, it is difficult for them to reestablish themselves in the mood proper for the mystery of the flow of creative power.

If I am such a man, I should feel obliged in conscience to be faithful to the Spirit and to decline participation, even on a part-time basis, in the regular parish work to which my fellow religious may feel attracted. The same may be said for socializing or pastoral counseling if they would interfere with the highest contribution that I as a religious can make to the culture. I should pray humbly for the courage to resist any disrespectful infringement upon the personal, essential availability which I should be for the unfolding Holy, Who has called me to a specific cultural task which may exclude my involvement in regular parish care or pastoral counseling. I should pray especially for an awareness of my prepersonal, egocentric needs for popularity and esteem as an approachable, ever-available fellow. These needs more readily interfere with the recollection which may be necessary for me if I am called by the Spirit to serve His humanity in a creative way, a way which often requires relative silence and withdrawal from the crowd. Thus many creative priest-religious are called to sanctify themselves and their work by sharing in the suffering and misunderstanding of Our Lord. The relative seclusion and unavailability of a creative religious may be explained away as haughtiness, pride, insensitivity, and lack of fellowship by religious who have not been sufficiently formed in deep respect for the unique calling of their fellows. The lack of easy popularity and acceptance in his immediate environment is frequently the price the creative religious must pay for his unusual gift and its fruitfulness.

It becomes clear how fundamental it is to foster as many vocations as possible for the diocesan priesthood in both developed countries and mission areas. When the Church has at its disposal a sufficient number of diocesan priests, laymen, and women, she does not need to appeal to the participative religious to help out in the regular care of the daily spiritual needs of her faithful. In other words, the larger and more qualified the number of diocesan priests, and of members of diocesan lay institutes, the greater the number of religious who will be free to live the life of religious participation in the culture. Diocesan priests and priest-religious, therefore, should not compete with one another but complement one another. Both are engaged in worship, in the consecration of humanity to the Holy, in pastoral and religious care. Only the areas and modes of these priestly functions are different. This condition does not exclude that in times of need, members of one kind of clergy may take over the other's essential work. It means only that we should avoid the pitfall of ever defining the essence of the diocesan priesthood or that of religious life on the basis of temporal emergencies, even if these emergencies endure for centuries. The essential meaning of participative religious life can be understood neither from the essential orientation of the contemplative life, nor from the fulfillment of the temporary diocesan and missionary needs to which a considerable number of members of these participative communities at times dedicate themselves, nor from the essential aims of institutions which are directed toward the regular, systematic care of the general pastoral needs of members of the Church. To be a participative religious means to be present to the unfolding Holy in the culture as a unique person who fully participates in the inner orientation of his cultural endeavors according to his own personal affinity and the specific community to which he belongs.

4

Living The Participative Religious Life

As a participative religious I am called to show by the very mode of my participation that the world of culture is in truth one world with two aspects — one radiant and the other opaque. Indeed the deepest meaning of human culture may remain hidden by immediate appearances and by the manifold egocentric ways in which man manipulates cultural life for his own purposes. The luminous aspect of culture is the transcendent meaning of the unfolding of creation to which all cultural and social enterprises point. My calling is to help withdraw this veil of opaqueness by means of a selfless, deeply religious way in which I serve the cultural unfolding of mankind and world. In the midst of the visible culture I am a witness to its invisible core and to man's potentiality for transcendent openness. With my fellow religious I live among the people, sharing their cultural endeavors and striving for the supreme fulfillment of the culture in its transcendent meaning. I thus become indifferent to merely worldly success. Indeed, I learn to refuse success if it serves self-enhancement so as to betray the sacred inner dynamics of culture and cultural endeavor.

The area of culture in which a religious participant should worship and witness is dependent on his unique personality and life situation and determined in dialogue with his superior. He may be found among administrators, intellectuals, artists, technicians, laborers, nurses, teachers; or he may serve the poor, the pagan, and the oppressed in slums and ghettoes throughout the world. The religious is called to participate wholeheartedly in the manifold orientations of contemporary society. Such orientations are partly dependent on the actual stratification of the culture. Here we are concerned with the stratification of our Western society in which the aristocratic classes of former ages have been gradually replaced by professional classes. In the Middle Ages and the early Renaissance, stratification was based partly on birthright. There existed a small group of noblemen, a limited number of intellectuals, and a large, somewhat undifferentiated population of common men. Since those times, increasing specialization of functions has led to an increasing specialization of professions. Traditional social units, such as the village, the town, and the parish have been supplemented today by professional and academic groups of manufacturers, skilled laborers, technicians, doctors, scientists, artists and lawyers.

A major influence on the Western world has been the Christianization of society, or more precisely, the incarnation of Christ within the tradition and style of life of the units which make up society. The continued Christianization of humanity requires the incarnation of Christ in the new tradition, style and perspective of a society increasingly specified by professional, technical and academic dimensions. However, professional people may be so absorbed by their specialized interests that in many cases there is little time or energy left for the assimilation of other values. The greater part of their day may be spent within a special professional circle which cultivates a life perspective and often a language of its own. As a result, their daily mode of existence may be molded predominantly by professional experience which colors their life as a whole. This does not mean that the professional person is closed off from more fundamental modes of presence, but only that in our differentiated culture these modes are in danger of neglect.

Phenomenon of Religious Abandonment

Often in the past, groups of Christians, inspired by a prophetic leader, have emerged and concentrated their attention on a spiritually neglected sector of society. Frequently, they have called this field of preference "the abandoned souls" or "the apostolate for which it is difficult for the Church to find workers." Such dramatic terminology was in keeping with the spirit of times in which a patronizingly romantic and compassionate description of neglected groups was apt to open the hearts and loosen the purse strings of the faithful who financed the effort of Christian incarnation among such groups as laborers, pagans, the colored and the poor. Today "underprivileged groups" are more sensitive to their newly experienced human dignity and therefore less fond of the label "abandoned souls" or "apostolate for which the Church only with difficulty can find workers." The label, however, is secondary to the question of the phenomenon itself. What do religious communities basically mean when they designate "abandoned souls" as one of the available fields of action for their members, especially when the community desires to select its field of preference in the light of this meaning?

By abstracting as far as possible from all influences of custom, language habits, unconscious needs, and other incidental features due to circumstances of space, time and personality, I may derive the root meaning of this phenomenon. The expression itself refers to those units or dimensions of society in which Christianity is not yet present to such a degree and in such a way that Revelation can implicitly or explicitly permeate their tradition, style and culture. That the people concerned may be colored or poor, artistic or intellectual, peasant or bourgeois, country or urban dwelling, foreign or native, capitalist or communist is incidental and should not enter into a consideration of the fundamental structure of the phenomenon of *religious abandonment*.

The crucial question is not whether this dimension of society is artistic, scientific, or social, but that it is not sufficiently permeated by presence to the transcendent. Such presence reveals the internal sacred orientation of all cultural dimensions and leads to the fulfillment of creation — not only to the self-enhancement of the educator, laborer, social worker, administrator, scientist, nurse, or scholar. If there are not sufficient witnesses for the sacred inner orientation of a specific cultural field, it is a religiously abandoned field. The "souls" of those laboring within these fields, or of those touched by these fields, may be in danger of "abandonment" because their life orientation is potentially corruptible by a selfish abuse of their very professional and academic achievement.

The best indicator of the phenomenon of the absence of living Christianity is, therefore, not color, accent, or social status but the number and character of people who are no longer present to the sacred inner dimension of reality within a sector of the population or a field of cultural activity. In France this population may be the laborers; in Ireland, the playwrights, poets, and novelists; in South America, the peasants; in the United States, the leading philosophers, scientists, scholars, and artists. The fundamental phenomenon remains always and everywhere the same; its incidental aspects change with the conditions of time and space.

Characteristic of the United States, for example, is a concentrated presence of Christian tradition among the laboring and the industrial middle classes, with a far less intense representation among scholars, scientists, writers, and artists. There is an admirable effort in many religious communities to free their members for the assimilation of the culture, idioms, and customs of natives in foreign missions so that they may be able to communicate with them and to integrate Christ into their interests and traditions. There is perhaps less effort to free members of religious communities to assimilate the philosophical, literary, artistic, or scientific languages of the scholars, artists, scientists, and creative writers who set the tone of thought and feeling in our society. It is true that religious in many cases are stimulated to serve some educational institution by obtaining a master's or doctor's degree as quickly as possible. But often this study is done with the pragmatic purpose of obtaining the union card necessary for academic teaching. The degree, combined with a minimum knowledge of a field, makes a decent performance in teaching possible. But such a degree is only the most elementary beginning of entering creatively into the area of academic and professional dialogue in which the thought and the mood of our time are molded. It signifies that the religious witness has rudimentary tools which after one or two decades of intense use may lead to a knowledge which enables him to participate in an original way in the intellectual, literary, or artistic life of the nation and the world. In other words, the degree is a mere possibility for creative religious witnessing in a cultural field.

A comparison with the foreign missionary may illuminate what we mean. The missionary is not a man who over the years obtains some basic familiarity with the language, customs, and thought patterns of a tribe, and then returns to his former milieu to spend the rest of his life telling his companions all that he has learned in his glorious years with the natives. The authentic missionary generally sacrifices his own cultural background, perceptions, and prejudices to live in a foreign land and communicate for a lifetime with the people to whom he has been called. He assimilates continuously their evolving ways of thought and expression, and he becomes in some sense a native himself. He patiently discovers links between native tradition and Revelation which may enable him to incarnate Christ in his milieu. The fundamental psychological structure of the missionary comprises an unusual ability for decreasing affiliation with his own culture and increasing assimilation of another culture in order to fuse it with Christian Revelation. To be sure, not every religious has this special psychological inclination. Therefore, not every religious is called to the beautiful, unique life of the foreign missionary.

Something similar can be said of the religious called to the abandoned souls among the "tribes" of scholars, scientists, artists, and creative writers. To be sure, he does not enter into a culture totally new to him, as the foreign missionary does, but his witnessing may imply the assimilation of a subculture relatively foreign to him. The alarming lapse of sensitivity for the Holy in certain professional circles is even more tragic when we consider their constant influence on the mood, taste, and thought of increasing numbers of students and intellectuals in our society. In other words, the lapse of faith in these influential subcultures may gradually decrease the faith in the culture as a whole.

As we have said, groups of men and women in the history of the Church banded together under the inspiration of prophetic leaders in order to incarnate Christ in the culture of "abandoned souls" of their time. It was this phenomenon which usually prompted the emergence of new religious communities. Nevertheless, many of their saintly founders were inspired to provide also for members who desired to dedicate their lives to answering the call of the Holy in activities different from the field of preference of their foundation. Often their successors failed to develop the same degree of relaxed sensitivity and obedient openness to the inspiration of the Spirit in each individual member. There are instances in which, after the death of the founder, the field of preference developed itself into a powerful monolithic enterprise. The majority of members identified with this field and elected leaders among themselves whose interests and actions promised the greatest development for the particular enterprise which put the community "on the map" in the first place. Naturally such leaders were tempted to listen more to the concrete systematic needs of the establishment than to the possible whisperings of the Holy Spirit in those members who, while perfectly at home in religious life, did not adapt well to the type of work preferred by the majority. Instead of living in a relaxed flexible openness for the Holy, these leaders hardened their hearts so that they forced each man and woman into the established system of operation, even when it was perhaps impossible for some members to live balanced, serene, and creative lives within the confines of these works. Being faithful to their religious vows, they had no choice but to live the major part of their lives in works for which they felt no inclination.

Another typical hardening of position, sometimes linked with the above symptoms of ossification, is even more directly relevant to our topic. Frequently, in the course of history, a fixation of perception on incidental features of the phenomenon of "abandoned souls" ultimately defeats the original fundamental principle of selection. Accidental features of the phenomenon of religious abandonment such as skin color, the peasant way of life, slum dwelling, or unpolished language sometimes become the main cause for charitable and apostolic attention. Naive religious communities may be tempted to confuse *material* abandonment with *religious* abandonment. While it is undoubtedly true that these two may be found side by side, they are not identical.

This somewhat romantic distortion of how abandoned souls appear outwardly may be harmful to

Christianity, especially when such naive romanticism directs the selection of fields of preference for the majority of religious communities. While congregations which are faithful to the essence of religious life will always encourage members with a different inspiration to follow the voice of the Spirit in their lives, it is obvious that the greater majority of their members will still be most at home in the specific fields made available by the community. Practically, this means that the selection of fields of preference in the light of the principle of "abandoned souls" by so many religious communities is bound to leave fields that are judged not to be "abandoned" with only a small number of religious who feel inspired by grace and disposition to be present in those areas which do not fall under the fields of preference of their communities. But this is not all. Because of a materialistic fixation on bodily or material signs of abandonment, the majority of religious communities may distort the phenomenon of "abandoned souls" and indeed may overlook a group of the population which is actually most abandoned.

Even priests and laymen who do not belong to any of these religious communities may be fixated in the same manner, so deeply impressed are they by the constant projection of the material needs of certain segments of the population, for which the communities understandably need money, support, and vocations. The paradoxical situation thus arises that certain groups of the population which may be in fact most abandoned religiously are not reached by a sufficient number of priests, religious, and laymen. One reason for such neglect is that they do not strictly fulfill the presupposed material signs of religious abandonment, such as skin color, decaying dwellings, or a low degree of civilization.

It may be objected that the incarnation of Christ in cultures and subcultures should be served by laymen only. Instead of saying by laymen only, I should prefer to say that the incarnation of Christ in the culture should be served by laymen mainly. Not only are they called as Christians to permeate the culture with the Revelation of Christ, but their sheer numbers enable them to reach a larger segment of the culture. Nonetheless, the vital presence of the participative religious remains desirable in every culture and subculture. He is the man set free from the regular spiritual and material care of the people of God in the familial and diocesan systems which maintain Church and society. This unique freedom makes possible the creative commitment of his whole being, and the direction of all his energy and attention toward the Incarnation of Christ within the various subcultures and professions. The religious should be present not only by his own immediate participation in the cultural task concerned, but also as a source of religious inspiration for those laymen who engage with him in a specialized dialogue. Scholarly and professional laymen may wish to discuss their problems of integration of religion and culture with a religious who, by personal inclination and grace, by training, prayer and recollection, can fully participate in the highly specialized dialogue between Revelation and culture.

Unfortunately, however, the body-mind dualism of Descartes still poisons the thought of many religious. One of its harmful symptoms is the schizoid opinion that only laymen should assimilate the style, thought, and feeling of the various subcultures, such as those of the Negroes, the farmers, the artists, or the scholars; that only laymen should be present among these populations, while religious should pray, teach catechism to all, and do pastoral counseling without involvement in any subculture. Revelation must be communicated, however, to living people who exist in a variety of subcultures. The subculture is not separated from their personalities but permeates them to such a degree that it is their very being. Moreover, a religious is presence to the culture too. This means that he cannot live as a religious witness without participation in the subculture to which he is called to be a witness. If I as a religious refuse to participate wholeheartedly in this reality, I may fail to communicate Revelation through culture. I should strive to present Revelation in the style of the subculture to which I am sent. There is no choice for me between culture or no culture. To be man is to be cultured in some way. I am compelled either to assimilate the subculture of the academic, professional, or ethnic group to which I am committed or to impose Revelation upon them in the style of the subculture of my own family, or of a particular convent-culture which I may have developed in my years of religious life. Both of the latter subcultures may be foreign, or even repulsive, to people who belong to the particular subculture which I am called to serve. Most harmful would be the implicit suggestion that the subculture of my own family or of my specific religious community is part of Divine Revelation itself. As a religious, I should not set myself apart from the culture but should adapt my subculture and style to those of the people entrusted to my care.

Again, the professional and academic stratification of contemporary Western society confronts the religious community with a unique problem. Society, as we have said, formerly consisted of a few large subcultures, each one relatively homogeneous, sharing one tradition and perspective. The religious community could then prepare future individual witnesses for the

Holy to be present to *the* laborers, *the* aristocracy, or *the* farmers. We still find these large segments in our society. But the trend is unmistakably toward the increasing development of a variety of vocational, professional, and academic superstructures, each with a different life style and perspective. Each of these superstructures should have its religious witnesses for the Holy. This is true first of all for the large groups of laborers, teachers, nurses, office workers, and industrialists. But it is also true for superstructures in which relatively few people are called to live, such as those of the artists, creative scholars, and university professors. These groups represent minorities sharing the same unusual intellectuality, aesthetic sense, and creativity. Such people, living unusual vocational superstructures, are likely to become the most "abandoned souls" if the few religious like them are not allowed to share their vocational life. Religious who fulfill the conditions for efficient presence in these groups are rare on the statistical scale. There may be few in an entire community. Therefore, a generous concentrated effort of *all* religious communities is needed to make these gifted few available to meet their cultural partners in their highly specialized fields.

People with special ability for original scholarship or artistic creation will always be scarce on the normal distribution curve of the abilities of the general population. This curve also applies to the population of a religious community. While it is true that the all-powerful grace of God can transcend the limitations of human abilities, it is also known from history that grace does so only in very exceptional cases. Therefore, it is not probable that God by a special miracle will suddenly transform a large number of religious into Shakespeares, Einsteins, Picassos, or Pasteurs. The slogan of many religious communities, *paratus ad omnia* — "ready for everything" — would be meaningless if it were translated as meaning that we find in the nature of each religious, or in his personal calling, an ability for the excellent fulfillment of every possible task in society. Simple observation teaches us that each religious has not the capacity to be a poet, painter, administrator, university professor, or skilled manual laborer. Readiness on the part of the religious, therefore, does not guarantee capacity for all achievements. Consequently, I act unwisely when I desire an appointment which I cannot fulfill in spite of my best intentions and desires. To promote true self-realization in witnessing for the religious dimension in our culture, superiors must be aware of opportunities to place their religious in cultural positions in which their personalities and talents can be best utilized, even if these works happen to be outside the preferential field of activity of the community. Superiors can discover these unique opportunities only through constant dialogue with the culture and with the religious concerned.

This concept does not eliminate at all the possibility that such a "readiness of the will" may mean my sacrificing other possibilities that seem to me more interesting. I may have abilities for a variety of endeavors, some of which I like very much while others are less to my liking. Nonetheless, I should maintain a readiness of will to commit myself to that task which seems, in the light of my dialogue with my superior, most in tune with the concrete life situation in which I find myself, even if I should have preferred some other work of which I feel equally capable.

We may return now to the problem of the few who are able and willing to witness for the Transcendent within highly specialized milieus. These artists, scientists, and scholars are sometimes persons who pay for their special gift with considerable limitations in other practical areas of life in which they may well be mediocre, clumsy, and naive. In other words, a highly specialized capacity in one area of life may entail a remarkable lack of ability in certain other areas. Unable to accept a particular limitation in his profile of abilities, the religious may try out all kinds of tasks in which his fellow religious are proficient, only to discover painfully how awkward he is in simple matters of daily life. His difficulties may be aggravated if his superiors or fellow religious resent the fact that his special gift of God is to be good at painting, poetry, or the pursuit of scholarship. All the community, including the one-sidedly gifted religious himself, may be severely tempted to improve on the limited creation of God which he is. He, his fellow religious, and his superiors should nevertheless attune the readiness of their wills to the limited ability granted to him by God. In this special case, "readiness for everything" implies a humble acceptance of the fact that the ability of this particular religious may be limited to only one area. On the other hand, this very limitation may facilitate the generous willingness of the community to make the unusually gifted person available as a religious witness within his special field.

A general refusal by religious communities to release their members for those areas in which they are best qualified to serve, whether social or intellectual or aesthetic, will necessarily lead to the continued absence of Christianity in these subcultures. Social life, art, science, literature and contemporary thought will then be molded without Christian witness. A culture may emerge which is incompatible with the Christian spirit. The Christian who lapses into a secular, profane state of mind will represent an increasing symptom of this tragic condition. It is as if Christ asks us, His religious, to allow Him to incarnate Himself through our work among the least recognized "abandoned souls." A community's generous readiness to allow certain members to dedicate themselves to the difficult, often painful dialogue with subcultures more alienated than others from the religious dimension of life should represent a consent on the part of all members. True community spirit is absent if only a few superiors or fellow religious support the lonely member who must represent the Holy in a cultural territory alienated from the sacred.

Community spirit implies that each member respect and support the cultural task of every other member. Generally speaking, the more specialized the position of a religious celibate in the cultural world, the more he needs the conviction that his fellow religious grant him the gifts of sympathy, respect, and understanding. Living and working in alien territory, he is likely to meet with distrust, antipathy, and suspicion. Faithful to his calling, he often does not enjoy the abiding respect which he would receive if he labored among the faithful in the regular care of parishes, Catholic schools, or other Church-related institutions. If he is the brunt of suspicion or malicious rumors in his own community, the fulfillment of his task will be much more difficult. He may be distinguished among his fellow religious because of his interaction with a suspected or even despised "out-group," or because of the new, strange language he is obliged to speak in order to communicate with this group, or because of unconscious jealousy and envy which may emerge when he is publicly acclaimed for some success in his field. Distrust may also breed among simple clergymen and Christians who accept the religious only within the confines of the regular care of the faithful through established parishes. They honestly believe there is something doubtful in his attempt to interact with people who are not baptized or to become involved in sciences and arts when all anyone has to do to save his soul is to go to Church. Well meaning, simple people like these may be scandalized by the unique cultural task of the religious in the world. Their condemnation may even influence the community which the religious celibate who goes out into the world of science and culture calls his home. To be sure, such suffering may sanctify the defamed religious, but it will do nothing to encourage other candidates to follow his endeavor. In other words, distrust, antipathy, and misunderstanding may ultimately harm the essential orientation of the participative religious community, which should be ready to free for special witnessing the few who are able to serve the Holy in areas of the culture where the religious dimension is forgotten.

Circles of artists, creative scientists, scholars, and

contemporay philosophers may represent foreign countries to be reached only by similarly gifted religious sent by their communities not to preach but to engage in dialogue. This crucial dialogue of our times does not aim primarily at making converts, or spreading propaganda for the community, or increasing its power and prestige. Rather, it aims at laying the groundwork for a new integration of the sacred and the profane, an integration through which humanity may find a new openness toward the Sacred without feeling compelled to deny the authentic advances of its cultural and functional modes of being. Once this openness is created and maintained by religious witnesses and their fellow Christians, modern society may be able to hear again the voice of the Lord. So long as the lonely witness for the Holy does not succeed in the religious integration of both his special field and its cultural participants, he will remain a citizen of two countries. He accepts this marginal position for the love of Christ, so that the light of Revelation may permeate a culture and tradition where it was absent before he was present. He does not experience the satisfaction of the successful convert-maker. He simply engages in a dialogue which makes Revelation present in the modern world; he may never live to see the fruit of his endeavors.

Participative Religious Awaken the Potential Worshipper in Others

No matter where I am called to witness, my transcendent openness is initially invisible to the people around me. When I participate in the culture as a laborer, nurse, poet, scholar, teacher, or administrator, it is not immediately evident that in and through my task I worship and witness for the Holy. This worship is first of all an interior attitude whose subtle exteriorization in my behavior can be discovered only at the moment that the other is also open to the need for worship in his own personality. People may rub shoulders with me every day without recognizing the true meaning of my life. The important thing, however, is that my life remains the visible actualization of my fellowman's own deepest potentiality for presence to the Holy in and through the daily task.

As a religious witness, I may appear as an average man, seemingly absorbed in the most common endeavors. My outward life may seem to consist of a series of dull and monotonous acts; now and then, a familiar gesture of mine may reveal in the most natural way the religious inspiration which sustains me in my daily contribution to the unfolding of God's world. A word, an understanding look may suddenly transform the vision that my cultural participants have of my life and bring them into touch with their own call to transcendent presence. Through worship I transform the meaning of cultural life into a gift and a call of the Holy. Without disturbing in any way the natural aspects of each cultural enterprise, this call of the Holy shines through and reveals itself to man as precisely that aspect of his task which grants him serenity of heart and strength of will, enabling him to serve the unfolding culture in a most effective and selfless way. Through this transcendent presence to his daily cultural task, man transforms not only the earth but also himself. In the course of his daily transcendent dedication to his calling as guardian and originator of culture, he discovers his best and holiest self.

My cultural participant is also called to live his task in religious presence. I am called to assist him by my very mode of cultural participation in his struggle to be born as a *religious* guardian and initiator of culture. To be sure, the recognition and fulfillment of this call is a grace which I cannot compel and which continually resists my willfulness. Therefore, I must never be impatient. Impatience is an insult to the Holy who in His own way and time will grace man with religious presence. I should be serenely satisfied with a daily growth in religious presence to my task, whether or not the Holy chooses to use my efforts to awaken my cultural partner to his own call to grace. Even when the Holy calls him, I should still consider myself a useless servant. My duty is simply to do my best to keep religious participation alive in me. On the other hand, I share all the weaknesses of my cultural participants in the world. I am in no way stronger than they; and some of them may be far more religious in their cultural presence than I shall ever be. The difference between them and me is that I have been called specifically to develop my religious awareness unburdened by the myriad functional preoccupations which would be mine if I were called to care for a family or to work under the absolute rule of social or diocesan establishments. I have been called to this specific freedom of the spirit not for my own sake, but in order to witness for my fellowman that cultural presence should be a religious presence too. The ground of my call is a free gift of God; it is not granted because I am holier or more open by nature to religious experience than my fellowmen. There may be people far holier than I, exceptionally graced and gifted men and women, more open than I shall ever be to religious experience, who are not called to live the religious life but to live their presence to the Holy in an *extraordinary* way as laymen in the world. They are exceptions. But neither the life of the layman nor that of the religious should be evaluated in the light of the small number of *exceptionally* graced and gifted persons whom we may find in both.

The meaning and possibilities of both ways of life should rather be appreciated in the light of the average human beings who populate the social systems and establishments in the world as well as the religious communities. If I should take a sample of the average population (for example, each tenth man or woman in a busy international airport), I should find in the significant majority of cases that it is more difficult for these average men and women to keep open to the transcendent meaning of their cultural tasks than it is for each tenth religious in a community. Nevertheless, each one of these laymen is called and has the potentiality to live his daily task in worship. He needs, however, the presence of witnesses for this openness to the Holy so that he can experience in a moment of grace what the deepest meaning of his daily task is. Therefore, the Holy calls forth out of their midst men and women, average for the most part, who create a special life situation which frees them from many occupations which might obscure the transcendent meaning of the cultural tasks. This freedom enables these average men and women to live a life of worship and witness more intensely than would have been possible had they not been set free by vows from many functional and emotional cares.

As a participative religious, I should share the cultural dedication of my fellowmen so deeply that they will often fail to recognize me as a religious. I shall not be among them as an example of pure perfection, but as someone whom they can see and touch, whose weaknesses and foibles they can observe, and whose life is involved in their lives of cultural dedication. I am not a pure spirit. As a participative religious, I have dedicated myself to a life of everyday cultural endeavor, together with the men and women who maintain and create this world. It is true that I should be in communion with God, but precisely because I do live in communion with God, it should be easier for me to live in communion with the cultural unfolding of man and the world as the very manifestation of God. Each aspect of my cultural task is an opportunity to be used, an invitation of the Holy to give myself without reservation. I should be involved in my personal cultural calling so spontaneously and naturally that I make this task radiant and meaningful, where it might have seemed a drudgery, relatively meaningless and isolated from the sacred meaning of life and history. It will be especially striking to people around me when I do not give the impression that I have renounced human nature, eradicated my natural likes and dislikes, repressed my personal failings, or overcome the passions present in every human being. My companions will discover that I can be elated and depressed, angry and aggressive. I should not repress these feelings, for they remain a condition of my full enthusiastic participation in the unfolding culture.

Religious participation is itself a passion, a humanized and graced passion. There is in passion a power which I as a religious witness need in order to resist the drives for status, possession, and popularity which prevent man from being faithful to the inner, sacred orientation of cultural enterprises. It is passion which stimulates and raises me to higher levels of presence to my cultural task. On the whole, those of us who build the world may be inclined to be content with a mediocre life, with the complacent, commonplace meaning of our task as a service of temporal interest. But what should mark the religious witness is his passionate readiness to serve the culture within his specific task to the limit of his powers. My involvement in the culture should be vital and spontaneous because of its closeness to the movement of my personality as a whole and to the dynamic forces from which spring cultural acts and creations. Therefore, I do not fight my natural impulses; rather, I find in them the source of my enthusiastic engagement in the culture. Instead of diminishing the divine gift of my natural impulses and passions, I direct them with God's grace to their final end, so that they may enable me to be a stimulated and stimulating participant in the cultural unfolding of God's presence in the world. In this very process of transcendence, impulse, desire and passion are sublimated under the impact of grace. This transcendence of the limits of my nature does not destroy my inner purpose; on the contrary, it helps me to reach more fully and effectively the end to which my nature as gifted with impulse and passion is striving.

As a religious participant in the world, I therefore do not repress or deny human feelings and excitement; I live these feelings to the full by directing them to fulfill their inner aspiration which cannot be satisfied with any achievement that is less than the best they can reach. If I, with God's grace, succeed sometimes in at least the approximation of this fulfillment, my life of passion, desire and emotion finds its destiny.

All of us are prone to be blinded by the need for status, popularity, and possessions; we are prone to debase and degrade the powers which nature and culture have made available to us. Both the divine and the demonic in my life thrive on the same dynamic powers in my personality, but it is only in the life of the Spirit that nature and culture find their true fulfillment and highest unfolding. The true religious is not a man engaged in a relentless war against the structures of nature and culture, for the natural unfolding of man in and through culture comes from God. As a cultural-religious participant, I must make visible to the world that the highest development of culture is possible only in the light of its transcendent meaning; as a Christian religious, I must make visible that it is ultimately the supernatural which gives each aspect of culture its fullness and significance.

5

Religious Community

To be a religious is to be called to live in a unique and personal way my presence to the Holy as the hidden source of true unfolding in the world. In accordance with my personal history, education, and interests, I share joyfully in the ongoing struggle of mankind. I may share in this involvement of man and world as a housecleaner, administrator, poet, laborer, painter, social worker, architect, teacher, nurse, scientist or scholar. No matter what I am called to be, I shall answer this call as a religious from the viewpoint of my presence to the unfolding Holy as manifesting itself in the flow of man's development and in my unique affinity to one or the other aspect or phase of this human evolution.

While these various participations in human becoming are holy insofar as they bring to fruition God's creation, they may be lived in unholy ways. Contemporary man finds himself inserted in a complex historical and sociological situation rewarding and promoting his compliance and complicity. I cannot deny that such a setting is necessary for the maintenance of certain values and institutions; but neither can I deny the possibility that conformity to certain aspects of the established order may curtail a person's potential to realize the best and most creative aspects of his profession. Likewise, this same order may lead to a self-centered concern for his position. For example, a university professor who feels that he should forge a new direction in his field may choose instead to obsequiously follow established norms because it is safer, pays better and is less risky for his status and chances of promotion. Such an attitude may be unholy and even sinful; however, it is also possible that the pressure of family care compels him to pay homage to the established structure.

As a celibate religious, I am called to be relatively free from the potentially destructive power of social systems and establishments so that I may better serve their original holy purpose and realize their sacred direction, even though this freedom may imply less promotion, status, and popularity. In other words, my freedom from family responsibility mitigates the potentially corrosive power which the systems or establishments in which I work possess over me. While some persons may live their celibate religious life alone, I, as an average man, am better able to do so with the encouragement, protection, and sustenance of other religious called as I to dedicate themselves to the cultural fulfillment of creation as a revelation of the Holy. It is, therefore, quite natural that celibate religious come together and form communities. If we are to see a community of religious celibates as something original and unique among the forms of community known in culture and history, we clearly need a deeper insight into the true meaning of religious community.

I may have heard and possibly used flowery metaphors to express the similarity between the religious and other forms of human community. Traditional spiritual writers love to speak of religious community as a true family, a band of brothers or sisters lovely to behold, a holy army for Christ, a society, a new country or a heavenly Jerusalem. Metaphorical comparison, taken literally, may harm my wholesome development in religious life. I am bound to experience that my religious community can by no stretch of the imagination be a family; that we are by no means brothers or sisters, or even friends in the intimate sense; and that together we are least of all a heavenly Jerusalem.

If I read these metaphors as accurate descriptions of community life, I am bound to be disappointed. My vain attempt to live them day by day is unrealistic.

It forces me to falsify my situation — to role play *as if* we were real brothers, business partners, intimate friends, army buddies, or angelic spirits residing in heavenly realms. Such pretenses lead necessarily to mutual deception, loss of forthrightness, and repression of the awareness of our real feelings about one another. Taken literally, such metaphorical comparisons of religious community may even lead me to deny its deepest meaning, which is to sustain and promote the religious celibate's personal, independent and unique position of worship and witness in the world. Forced role playing robs me of my honesty and wholeness, weakens me and inclines me to be conformistic and deceptive, not only within my community but also in my participation in the culture. Attitudes and habits which I assume in daily interaction with my community tend to carry over into my life outside the community. It is thus vitally important that I perceive the singular character of the religious community as distinguished from the several forms of community mentioned here.

Community and Family

Some people parallel the members of a religious community and the brothers and sisters of a family. Brothers and sisters in a family are in need of physical care, education, and loving parental supervision. Parents protect and prepare their children in such a way that at some future date they will be able to leave the family and live independently. Another aspect of being brothers and sisters is one of commonality. Insofar as they are born of the same parents and have lived together from earliest years in similar surroundings, they share a cultural heritage, certain common customs, appreciations, evaluations and feelings.

In respect to both protective care and commonality, a religious community is the opposite of a family. Ideally, its members are mature men or women who have already found themselves and their unique, independent stand in the world. They do not live together to be made ready to leave the community once they are mature. Moreover, religious celibates do not necessarily share a similar family background. They may come from diverse levels of the population, manifesting an astonishing variety of national, cultural, and educational interests, personality traits and talents. This diversity may enable the community to provide the surrounding culture with personal witnesses for the Holy in every situation and profession. Where the life style of the family is more intimate, uninhibited, and mutually dependent, the life style of a religious community appears as necessarily more restrained and respectful. What should strike the outsider when he comes to know a religious community is not the relative sameness which he finds in a family, but a surprising uniqueness of personalities, interests and capacities through which the infinite richness of the presence of Christ may increasingly reveal itself in the culture.

The aim of the community can never be the community itself, no more than the aim of the family can be *per se* the family. Such self-centeredness would make the religious community another isolated system or subculture next to the numerous systems and subcultures which make up society. On the contrary, the ultimate aim of the religious community as community is to disappear as much as possible into the background, thereby granting its members increasing freedom for the pursuit of their personal religious presence in the social structure to which they have been called by grace, usually in accordance with their own predispositions. The authentic religious community repeats joyfully and humbly the words of St. John the Baptist, "He must increase and I must decrease." In this case, the personal presence of Christ in each member to the culture must increase, and preoccupation with the glory of the institute must decrease. The religious institute does not exist primarily for its own status and power but for the personal presence of Christ in the world. It exists, so to speak, to make each member increasingly free to realize his own unique potentiality to worship and witness in and through the culture.

Community and Friendship

Neither can a religious community be an association of friends in the strict sense. Friendship is a gift that cannot be forced. It is a rare event which occurs only when subtle psychological conditions are fulfilled. One of these is a certain affinity between the persons who become true friends. The celibate religious may or may not be so blessed that he will find, either inside or outside his community, a person with whom he has such an affinity. But, as we have stressed, religious celibates do not form communities on the basis of such rare affinities. On the contrary, the need of Christ for a diversity of personalities to carry on His mission among men may make it less probable that members of the community manifest an unusual affinity. What we as religious have in common is the same divine call to worship and witness for the presence of the Holy in some aspect of the progress of mankind, according to our personal talents and inspirations. To pretend that we necessarily share or should share one another's natural interests and predilections is to falsify the religious community by arousing unrealistic expectations, false guilt feelings, and disappointments. It is possible that we who share the call to witness for the Holy may not share any other psychological or cultural characteristics. This is one reason why the community is able to sustain the celibate's personal calling only when life can be lived in respected privacy within the community home. This aspect of religious life is evidenced in the great care communities take to provide for private rooms for each member and, if possible, private bathing facilities. It is also expressed in provisions for each member to have the use of his own books and supplies. Another evidence is the custom never to open another's correspondence unnecessarily and to provide, in accordance with one's assignment, private means of communication and transportation.

The religious community is a home in which mature persons enjoy as much privacy as is compatible with the maintenance of a fundamental structure of religious community life. This fundamental structure finds its temporal or local expression in community times or places for prayer, meals, and recreation, and in community services such as laundry, mailing facilities, and the common purchase of articles which are not by their nature personal and private. These arrangements are made in such a way that they help the religious to maintain and renew his personal inspiration. In being freed from as many daily functional cares as possible, he is made more free to pursue his cultural-religious task in the world.

Community and Company

If the religious community is neither a family nor a benign association of intimate friends, it is even less a task-oriented enterprise or company. The aim of the company is the good of the company; it serves society and in the process expands and enriches itself, gains status and recognition, and when possible, becomes a dynamic power in its own right. The essence of a religious community, on the other hand, is that it does not exist for itself, or for its own name and influence, but for the world. Therefore, the religious community is ideally indifferent to wealth, status, and power; it has no vested interests and does not strive for fame and recognition. Possessions which the religious community does not need for its survival, or for the needs of the present or future, are used for the personal development of the individual religious celibates and for the progress of the special tasks in which they are called to witness Christ's presence to the world.

Again, the company or productive institute is not primordially interested in its employees or their specific situation in the world. Its primary interest lies in the development of its own enterprise. Employees agree to join this enterprise and to work for its financial success, of which they too will receive a just share. Naturally and necessarily the company enterprise comes first; the personality, inspiration, and unique destiny of the employee are only secondary. Again the religious community is precisely the opposite. It is quite possible, and even advisable, that a religious community establish certain works for the many members who do not feel attracted to a lonely worshipping and witnessing of Christ in some specific realm of the culture. A certain religious community may, therefore, maintain schools and hospitals, or engage itself in pastoral occupations in parishes, missions and dioceses. But even in these enterprises the work is secondary to the individuals carrying it out. It just so happens that most religious men and women prefer an existing common enterprise to private witnessing. But the possibility must remain that those who are occupied in the ordinary diocesan or cultural systems may discuss with their superiors the desirability of leaving such work under obedience if they have serious reasons to do so. For it is the nature of religious life to make it *impossible* for any system or enterprise to ever *totally* dominate the religious community and the personal destiny of any one of its members. Religious life is essentially the liberation from the absolute domination of systems in order to serve mankind in the light of a transcendent presence to the unfolding Holy in the culture. The religious community is interested primarily not in the community as such, nor in any one of its common enterprises, but in its individual members, for it is only through them and their total response to the call of the Holy that the community will remain faithful to its original promise and destiny.

A company is a structural organization built rigidly around its specific production or assignment in society: to manufacture automobiles, to refine oil, to provide intricate parts of machinery. The life of the employees is directed in accordance with these objectives. In an analogous way, historical situations may have led religious communities to forsake temporarily the individual destinies of their members and to adopt in a more exclusive way a specialized enterprise in one field of action. The life and destiny of their celibates may have been decided by this specific assignment, whether it was cultural, pastoral, missionary, or diocesan. Such a situation, if fostered exclusively, has potentially far worse implications than the company-employee relationship. For a company has only partial power over the lives of its workers. Outside company time, they lead their own lives and fulfill their own destinies. A religious community, on the other hand, may subvert the entire life of its members to the tyranny of one binding enterprise. Thus the liberation from cultural and societal systems by means of the three vows may become a cruel irony. Before we realize what has happened, the purpose of being a religious may be perverted in such a way that the pastoral or cultural, the missionary or diocesan organization and its needs, practically dictate what should be done with the life of each member. If such is the case, the religious celibate could well have become a diocesan priest totally inserted in a system of pastoral care; or the sister could have become a teacher totally inserted in a diocesan or missionary organization, caring for certain specified needs under the well organized outlines of local authorities. We do not imply, of course, that the diocesan priesthood or womanhood serving within such systems is not fulfilling an admirable vocation, or that their task is any less necessary for the expression of the Holy in our culture. We only wish to emphasize that this work is not the essence of the religious vocation, for such a vocation implies a freedom and availability for the spirit and is to be distinguished from the lifelong vocation to the systematic care of established pastoral, social, charitable, and cultural endeavors. Religious can of course participate in such work, even in great numbers, but always under the condition that none of these enterprises ever totally dominates the freedom of the religious community and its members. No religious community can ever be identified unconditionally with any outside work or system and still maintain its freedom as religious community. As soon as it becomes identified with systematic enterprises, the question is raised by many: Why should we have specifically religious communities of priests, brothers, and sisters to serve these enterprises?

As we have said, the ideal religious community is a home which sustains and promotes the religious celibate's specific participation in the progress of mankind. It may happen that the community makes available certain common tasks, such as education, hospital care, pastoral counseling, or general parish or mission work, for those who otherwise may not find a congenial employment, or who do not have special preferences. However, the deformation of religious communities into task-centered companies occurs when such pastoral or cultural work becomes the vested interest of the religious congregation concerned; when everyone is *a priori* forced to be employed in such structures even when his personality, interests, and inspiration are directed elsewhere. The essential aim of a religious community is to foster the deeply personal religious orientation of its celibates and to enable them to be original participants in the world.

Community and Subculture

A religious community is not to be likened to a new country, a strange and isolated subculture, or a new class of people. In feudal periods such distortion of the religious life may have been a fact; today it belies the essence of the participative religious community to attract special attention by setting up its own celibate culture, or its own religious peculiarities, like a foreign culture within a culture. It is not the proper task of the religious celibate to stand out as an awkward, uncomfortable resident of another universe, or even worse, as a dignified unapproachable anachronism. Instead of helping cultured men to appreciate their own life style and occupation as potentially sanctifying, I become a witness for an artificial split between life and religion, culture and sanctity, progress and holiness. Rather, I should be a relaxed, spontaneous participant in the ongoing cultural-religious progress of humanity, neither arousing undue wonder nor fading dully into the background.

My community impresses on me from the beginning that I should experience any alienation from mankind as a sin against love and as an escape from my participative religious vocation. The religious community is distinguished by its honest attempt to make its members increasingly ready for full participation in the cultures and subcultures of society. The participative religious community as community attempts humbly to hide itself. It feels most successful when its members splendidly succeed as individual witnesses for Christ in the subcultures, professions, and enterprises to which they are committed, even when this means that the community itself may be increasingly unnoticed and forgotten. Such is the spirit which should guide the authority in a religious community. For as soon as this authority becomes concentrated merely on the fame, works, finances, status, influence, and power of the community as community, it is no longer able to bless the individual development of its members. Then both advice and decision always tend to be poisoned by community-centrism, a shared form of group egoism.

Community and Fraternity

Comparing the religious community to a fraternity, as we have compared it to a family and a company, makes clear from another perspective what a religious community *is not.* Fraternities are primarily interested in fostering social togetherness. While it is true that a religious community should provide a possibility for social life, especially for those who because of their specific personality structure need this kind of togetherness more than others, it is also true that concern for social life should never become a central one in the religious community. Too much social togetherness is detrimental to my personal development, to the depth of my prayer life, and to my potential for creativity, all of which demand silence and recollection.

When pleasant togetherness becomes an ultimate

criterion, the community falls easily into a mediocrity which repels mature individuals who are called by the Holy to become dynamic sources of thought and action in the culture. Such a perverted goal does not stimulate the pursuit of excellence. Instead, a cheap adjustment to the average begins to dominate community life and to destroy what should be a major concern for each person's unique field of attainment. A vulgar "regular guy" attitude may be substituted for sincere delight in the radical otherness of fellow religious. The hallmark of a true community is its ability to raise each individual member to the discovery and realization of his best and most singular capabilities. As soon as a religious community becomes indifferent to this goal, it may deteriorate into a sentimental crowd or a leveling collectivity without dynamism and inspiration.

Community and Army

Another favorite metaphor — also inaccurate — is to compare the religious community to an army. An army is built on the assumption that a first-rate power must have disciplined fighting men ready to defend its position if an emergency should arise. A catastrophic situation, such as enemy attack, leaves no time for individual deliberation. To cope with the danger of total destruction, the soldiers must act as the prolonged, united arm of the commanding general. In order to confront the worst that can happen, they are rigidly trained to execute each command without thought or hesitation. In the struggle for survival, it may be temporarily an absolute necessity for all individual needs, talents, thoughts, and projects to be submersed in the common movement of the army as a whole. Once biological survival and security are reestablished, the soldiers may return home and be themselves in those personal pursuits which always presuppose the emergence of the creative individual as individual.

Where the army is also characterized by its fundamental orientation toward conquest or defense, the religious community is in no way directed toward conquest or defense in the "enemy" territory of other religions or of non-believers. On the contrary, religious communities send their members forth as participants in the universal attempt of all mankind to better its condition. The contemporary religious should experience himself not as an aggressive or defensive soldier blindly inserted in the fighting unit of his religious community, but as a creative ally of mankind in its cultural-religious ascendance. The religious community is not a rigorously structured unit of warriors. It is a home of spiritual and human repose where the religious lives and deepens his presence to the Holy in order to be a more humble and loving presence to his fellowmen.

Community and Humanitarian Service

The religious community, moreover, cannot be likened to an association of humanitarians or social do-gooders. It is undoubtedly true that social care of the population and participation in the struggle for social justice are ways of serving humanity. However, this is not the only way in which the unfolding Holy inspires men and women to foster cultural progress. An interesting example can be found in the life of Vincent van Gogh, who mistook the call of the Spirit as a call to devote his life to socially abandoned groups of people in the mining country of Belgium. His genuine attempt to serve them led to personal disaster. Only when he discovered that the Spirit invited him to serve mankind through his remarkable paintings was he able to contribute effectively to the cultivation of humanity.

Perhaps one of the greatest temptations to misinterpret the voice of the Spirit in the religious community is the tendency of idealists to overwhelm others with their own excitement. It is natural, of course, that I express my enthusiasm for the field of cultural presence to which I am personally called. But I should realize that community life imposes on me an equally serious obligation to respect the possibility of other callings for other members. I should never proudly suggest that my type of service is holier than any other. Who am I to judge what is in the long run more crucial for the cultural-religious unfolding of mankind? I may silence the unique voice of the Spirit in others when I try to imbue them with *my* special social concern. I am especially prone to fall into this temptation when personally involved in exceptional social issues, such as missionary care in underdeveloped countries, working in the slums, or marching with people who seek social justice for minorities, or who desire the abolition of war. It may be that I am called personally to one of these specific ways of serving humanity, and my service is to be commended. But I should guard against the demonic pride which makes me disdain those who are called to serve the Holy, for example, as administrators, scholars, artists, musicians, or writers. To be sure, there are social and pastoral needs which should be administered in an organized way by certain groups of Christians. The diocesan priesthood and lay organizations are called to these regular tasks, and large numbers of religious may feel inspired to participate freely, either temporarily or lastingly, in the magnificent dedication of these admirable men and women. But it must never be forgotten that religious communities are first and foremost groups of individual men or women among whom personal freedom to follow the inspiration of the Holy under obedience is the first and foremost concern.

6

Community And Structure

The more we discover the meaning of participative religious life, the more we see emerging a general orientation toward a unique structure of presence. The structures which develop in a participative religious community are distinct from those which characterize any other kind of community. The specific orientation of this life necessarily colors its selection, initiation and elaboration of the possible structures open to man and human community. In the foregoing we have seen in different contexts what the participative religious community ideally should be. Now we may gather together some of these more salient aspects so that by their overall light we may see what should be characteristic of the structural orientation of participative religious community life.

Community Centeredness and Structure

As has been stressed repeatedly, a religious community does not have itself as its purpose; rather it attempts humbly to be an unnoticed background from which its members enter into the culture as individual worshippers and witnesses for the unfolding Holy. This is its most fundamental and basic orientation. If this is true, then I must say that every type of structuring which bends the participative community back upon itself is fundamentally false and will diminish, and possibly destroy, its essential meaning and mission. When a participative religious community starts to structure itself in ways that aim primarily at the assertion of its own status, power, or reputation, it removes itself and its members from the self-forgetful service of the Holy in the world. Rules, regulations, customs, and tyrannical expectations emerge which blight the full and honest presence of the individual members to the demands of true culture which is the unfolding Lord Himself.

This perversion of the community may taint each member. Instead of my asking in the light of the Holy Spirit what truly fosters the growth of the culture, or the development of the task in which I am involved, I may be inclined to ask first what is good for my community. How can I increase the name, power, and possessions of my community? Of course, I should not say that I have no responsibility to my religious congregation. All members of the community, in dialogue with their superior, should make sure that the necessary conditions for the maintenance of the community are fulfilled. Hence, there should exist a minimum of structures which guarantee the survival of the community as an agreeable, pleasant, and beautiful home that can fully care for the spiritual, social, educational, aesthetic and medical needs of the resident religious. My central attention, however, can never be for the community as such, but for the cultural-religious dimension of the world in which the community has allowed me to involve myself. Therefore, as a participant in such enterprises, my *primary* question should never be how does my work benefit my community, but how does it benefit the culture. I should also be careful never to tempt other members of the community to betray the essence of their vocation by suggesting that what the community obtains from a cultural-religious service is most important.

As soon as a participative community loses its fundamental orientation, perversion sets in and the consequences can be demeaning and disastrous. Each of us could give numerous examples. For instance, certain members of the community feel called by the Spirit to engage themselves in education — to participate in the unfolding Holy as it reveals itself in children, young men, women, or adults within the culture. With the permission of their superiors, they enter the field of education in elementary schools, high schools, colleges, or universities. If I am one of them, I am conscious of a sacred duty to serve the development of my students and to involve myself in the art or science in which the Lord desires my participation. It would be a betrayal of the Lord and His work if a self-centered community, or some of its members, would dare to suggest that we maintain a school primarily to secure vocations or to provide support for another work, such as the missions which bring traditional glory to our community.

How false is this readiness to put forth self-centered purposes of the community, or of the enterprises with which it proudly identifies itself, when I should be listening first to the inner demands of that school, those students, and that science or art. Communities which are perverted by self-interest may betray the true concerns of a field of culture or of the people entrusted to their care. Such side purposes always harm my full presence to the task at hand. Let us take another example. Suppose that I can reach more people in an unprejudiced openness to my scholarly discoveries if I do not put the initials of my religious order after my name because they may evoke prejudice in the readers of the journals concerned. Should I not omit these initials in order to serve better the unfolding of the Holy in my science or discipline? How strange it would be if my religious community, or one of its members, were more concerned about the reputation of the community than about the wider dissemination of scholarly knowledge among mankind. In their self-centeredness they would prefer the letters of the congregation after my name to the good which might be done for the Lord.

We should investigate all structures that exist in our communities in the light of the following criterion: Do they tend to keep the religious community in the background, as unobtrusive as is possible and yet compatible with the fulfillment of the necessary needs of the members of the community? Do these structures support as much as possible the fundamental orientation of the participative religious community: to make its members free as individuals for a task in the world which is not assumed primarily to enrich or to glorify the community itself but to make the Lord more present in all areas of our culture?

Work Structures — Religious Life Structures

Implicit structures which have not been codified often present more obstacles than structures which are officially written out. For example, certain pressure groups may have developed in the course of the history of a religious community. Such pressure groups may center around one or the other enterprise that a congregation makes available as a possible field of action for those members who do not manifest another special preference. These works may be schools, missions, hospitals, or pastoral activities. Usually a considerable number of members — probably the majority — engage themselves in these fields. This is not surprising, since many members predisposed to this type of common enterprise entered the community knowing that this kind of work would be open to them.

If pressure groups do not deeply understand the essential character of a participative religious community, and thereby the respect they must develop for each fellow religious and his possible inspiration, they may be inclined to identify such common enterprises with the religious community itself. Soon they may identify the virtue, glory, power and progress of the community with progress in the task in which the majority are successfully involved. Some members may be obsessed by a shared unconscious desire for advancement and achievement in the eyes of church and world. This desire easily tempts them to force upon others the drive which dominates their lives. They become oblivious to the principle that the authentic, primary aim of a religious order is never its power, success, and glory in one or the other field of common action with which it identifies itself. The aim of the religious community is to become increasingly the background from which individual men and women can emerge into the cultural world in which they will serve not the glory of their community or some of its more successful works but the glory of Christ.

It is also characteristic of the fundamental orientation of religious life to foster on all levels of structuring the individual presence of its members to the culture. This does not mean that an individual religious may engage himself in a whimsical way in every possible enterprise which strikes his fancy. The discovery of his life task should be the outcome of a dialogue with the proper authorities in which the persons concerned honestly attempt to discover *not primarily* what may advance the community, but in what way this unique individual can best participate in some area of the culture without harm to the minimum demands of the religious community.

The historical situation plays a major part in this decision. It is likely that my community in the course of history has become identified with certain cultural-religious works. Originally, the situation prompting these enterprises may have been very sound. It may have called for specific activities to answer specific contemporary needs. In no way, however, were these works intended to wield such a tyrannical hold over the life of the community and its members that no ground would remain for the inspiration of the Holy Spirit speaking in the uniqueness of each member and each group of members. It may unfortunately be the case that my congregation has identified to such a degree with certain specific enterprises that it is no longer clear whether the care for my personal and spiritual growth dominates the demands of the community on me, or whether the demands of the works to which the community is bound by history come first and foremost.

Realistically, I cannot expect my congregation to liberate itself overnight from exclusive care for a schocl system, mission, or chain of hospitals. Neither should I be surprised if its indigenous historical situation compels it to use me in a certain field of action even if I do not feel at home there. Nevertheless, while I and my fellow religious are not responsible for the formations of religious life developed under the past impact of historical needs or religious pressure groups, we are together responsible for the freeing of our religious life in the future from organizational influences which in their exclusiveness and absoluteness are obtrusively foreign to the internal orientation of the participative religious life.

Structures for Self-Renewal

My religious community should offer me a rich,

structured opportunity for prayer, recollection, and spiritual self-renewal, which are so necessary to foster my presence to the transcendent dimension of the cultural enterprises in which I am engaged. This is undoubtedly the most important service the community can render its members who return home from a great variety of enterprises in which they must frequently fulfill their tasks alone and even misunderstood by many. As a religious celibate, I am called to be present to my tasks and to people in a special way. Unencumbered by the care for a family, I must witness to the full the transcendent dimension of man's cultural enterprises. However, it is difficult — and for me as an average person almost impossible — to maintain such a motivation and such a presence if I live alone and am not constantly renewed, confirmed, and inspired by fellow religious who attempt to live the same kind of presence in perhaps totally different cultural enterprises. Therefore, as a religious celibate I need a community in which I can meet with others and together with them reorient myself in a fundamental way.

Here again we should carefully scrutinize customs, rules and regulations, asking ourselves whether they are most conducive to constant renewal of spirituality. It is true, of course, that spiritual life, in accordance with the potentially infinite richness of human existence, can be lived in many ways and styles, each with its own consistency and harmony. Therefore, we should have a variety of congregations, each of which has its own specific style of living this life. Then the special structuring of the spiritual life in each community will keep alive one of the many possible expressions of human spirituality and will attract those persons who are by their very dispositions more apt to benefit from this type of spirituality than from any other.

Politics and Careerism

Thus two essentials for sound structuring of the religious community are concern for daily regeneration of the spiritual life and for personal growth and development. These are endangered when self-centeredness or community-centeredness supersede authentic openness for the inspiration of the Holy Spirit. When the ultimate objective of the religious community becomes its own structures and strivings, the community begins gradually to bend back upon itself. When this happens, the greatest part of the energy and interest of the members is no longer invested in their task, but in their preoccupation with striving to gain positions of influence within their religious community or the enterprises that are completely under its control. Thus their primary question is no longer, how can I as a unique person best serve my Lord in the task which He has entrusted to me in the world, but how can I gain popularity, power, and influence within my community?

In other words, I may become more concerned about my career in the community than about my service to mankind. This preoccupation may lead me to engage in political maneuvers in order to gain positions of confidence and to foster my community career. I know that it is sometimes possible to play on the unconscious needs of my fellow religious who have important positions and to seduce them to grant me special favors by flattery or kind agreement even when I do not mean what I say. If I know how to play cleverly on the sentiments and insecurities of superiors and fellow religious — and especially if I have some talent for making a good impression — I can build a career for myself within my religious community or in the enterprises which are under its control. I realize very well that this manipulation would be more difficult if I were occupied in an outside field of cultural action, not owned or dominated by my community. There I would be obliged to produce concretely in order to be successful. With politics alone, I cannot go far in the world of fact and production; however, it is not always necessary to produce effectively within the religious community in order to climb the ladder of acceptance and confidence.

Once a religious community becomes increasingly introverted, the situation may become even more complicated. Various members who work at their careers begin half consciously to make connections with one another, or to develop informal groups of followers and sympathizers to sustain their growing influence. Soon the whole religious community may be busily preoccupied with schemes and counter-schemes, complaints and counter-complaints, gossip and rumors, political intrigues and pious power drives between various groups. Such community politics can absorb so much heated attention and agitation that very little energy is left for a serene presence to the Holy and for a full, unencumbered involvement in the cultural task. The introversion of the community has transformed it into a power constellation isolated from the world, a state within a state in which contesting groups, envious of one another's influence, engage themselves in the spread of rumors in service of their struggle for power and position. This perversion of the participative religious life reaches its apex when not only the fate of the community is affected by political games, but even the fate of the cultural fields of action in which the individual members are engaged. Soon the positions of the members in these enterprises are appreciated in the light of what their personal success can mean for the power struggle within the community. Religious who excellently serve the unfolding Holy in such fields may be destroyed or made suspect by religious careerists within the community. For the latter may feel or fear that such persons do not flatter them, or are not over-dependent on them, and therewith do not promote their own position of dominance. As a result, religious careerists may try to undermine successful fellow religious. In such cases, the cultural presence of a religious celibate may be destroyed because of the primacy of the inner power struggle within his community. The latter example represents an extreme form of perversion of the essential meaning of a participative religious community.

In short, just as self-centeredness is the beginning of the perversion of the individual religious celibate, so community-centeredness is the beginning of perversion of the common religious life. Both diminish selfless witnessing for Christ in the world by full participation in the cultural development of His redeemed humanity. The authentic religious community fiercely resists both self-centeredness and community-centeredness. Its strong resistance to any form of primary community-centeredness is inspired by its deep and abiding love for Christ, who steadily recalls the community from anxious self-preoccupation. The Holy Spirit incites the community to help its members replace self-centeredness and community-centeredness with a centeredness on the unfolding Holy in the culture. The first duty of the community is to discover and to obey the call of the Spirit by promoting each man or woman as a unique participant in one of the varieties of cultural trends, specializations, styles and enterprises wherein the Holy manifests itself. Therefore, a religious community should never be totally and exclusively identified with one type of work, with one class or group of the population, with one method of operation, or one style of expression. The worst thing that can happen to a religious community is to chain itself so fanatically to one type of systematized labor, be it pastoral or social, that its total orientation is enslaved to this enterprise.

Celibate Religious Life and the Structure of Community

It may be well at this point to emphasize the relationship between the individual celibate and the specific religious community to which he belongs. I must realize, first of all, how much we religious celibates living together are dependent on true respect for one another if we hope to faithfully fulfill our personal life vocations. If mutual respect and love does not steadily inspire us to support, encourage, and advance one another as unique individuals, some may suffer unjust cruelty from which there is no escape. For the inner attraction and divine calling binding us so deeply to this life means that outside it we would be unable to find fulfillment and joy.

When I experience the call to religious life, I also experience that I am not called to insert myself by means of a family into society. No matter how profound my reverence and admiration for the men and women who devote themselves to lifelong care for each other and their children, I know deep within me that I could never live that life without being untrue to myself as called forth from society and family to stand alone before the Lord and to participate in His culture as His special worshipper and witness. Neither do I feel attracted to the beautiful service of the diocesan priesthood. Listening to the voice of the Spirit within me, I am aware that I could not find personal happiness in the system of regular care of souls in a diocese or mission in the same way that a diocesan priest finds fulfillment in his life. I appreciate deeply what these men are doing, but I cannot escape the deeper attraction which I feel for the life of the religious. Its relative freedom from system offers more possibility for recollection and religious experience and gives me the opportunity, if I so desire, to be a witness for the Lord in a cultural-religious endeavor of mankind which does not totally and exclusively absorb me in a familial, diocesan, or missionary system.

This is not a question of greater holiness on my part. I realize that many fathers, mothers, and diocesan priests may be far holier than I shall ever be. The question is simply one of profound, almost irresistible attraction to a kind of life that does not *per se* make me holier but presents me with a different road toward holiness.

But how can an average person live such a life without contact with others who have the same calling, who are willing to encourage one another in this particular style of life, and who desire to create for one another spiritual and material conditions under which religious freedom from system and establishment is possible? I realize that persons who are above average spiritually and who are gifted in a very special way could live the life of religious celibacy independently, without the structures of a community. We know examples of lonely hermits who were able to live outside community, and of celibate laymen not called to marriage, who lived remarkable lives of religious witness in the service of their culture without developing peculiarities in their personalities in any way. No matter how deeply I admire them, I know before God that I could never risk living my religious celibacy out of touch with others who pursue the same freedom. I feel unable to bear the loneliness of a person who does not fit into the situational scheme of a society where everyone is more or less expected to do his duty by establishing a family and spending the better part of his energies in care for his wife and children. I also feel that it would be very difficult for me, who am not exceptional, to avoid idiosyncracies in my personality if it were not for the influence of the wisdom and tradition of my community, which follows the inspiration and experience of those who have tried to live this life for centuries. I alone, with my limited talents and capabilities, could never create the spiritual and material conditions for the religious freedom to which my heart goes out.

For all these reasons, my deepest longing compels me to enter a religious community. Where else could I go? I know that my fellow religious are bound to the community by the same inner necessity. Unable, with this specific attraction and supernatural call of Grace, to find fulfillment and happiness elsewhere in life, we feel compelled to participate in community life no matter how different we are from one another. Some of us are writers and artists, others are blessed with the gift of pastoral counseling, others are inclined to manual labor, to care of the sick, to social work, to missionary enterprises, to scholarship or science. But we all have in common the inner call to live a celibate life of religious worship and witness, and we all feel the necessity to live that life sustained by some type of community.

This necessity which we cannot escape should move us to allow as much leeway as possible for all of us to be ourselves. It would be of no avail if we were called from the systems and establishments of the world to find a more formidable power and a new type of strangling organization awaiting us. In this case, I should still feel that the deepest longing of my personality has not found possibility for fulfillment. And what makes it more painful is that outside the sustenance of my community I should not know where to go to be what God calls me to be. To be sure, I cannot expect the community to accept me without a commitment which guarantees that my desire to enter is not a temporary whim. Thus it demands that I solemnly commit myself to this freedom from systematic establishment and from family by religious vows. Through the vows I oblige myself to listen in obedience to the inspiration of the Holy Spirit in the culture as it comes to me in dialogue with my superiors; to keep myself free from the obligations which go with the establishment of a family or the promise of any other exclusive lifelong emotional involvement; and to abstain from the establishment and administration of a personal monetary enterprise which would link me in myriad ways to existing social and cultural systems and institutions.

Specificity of Structure

Ordinarily I shall prefer the specific structuring of one community over another as being more in tune with my personality. This specificity of structure is usually determined by two characteristics. First, the particular spirituality of my community is offered to me as a way of working out a mode of religious-cultural presence. Many modes are possible, and I feel initially in need of some model which is in tune with my personality structure and my culture as I experienced them before entering religious life. Not being a genius, nor a person extraordinarily enlightened by grace, I feel unable to develop a sound spirituality of my own without some model that has been traditionally developed in a specific community.

The community also makes available to me certain fields of action in cultural-religious areas in which its members have experienced how to serve in religious witness to the Lord. As I felt the need to be initiated in the spiritual life through the mode of spirituality developed by a community, so also I feel the need to be initiated in the art of religious participation in cultural endeavors. For many this will be accomplished by means of the works which the community makes available.

Initiation in a specific spirituality does not mean that I shall never grow beyond the model. My religious community desires to introduce me into the life of the spirit. While most religious may find fulfillment in the traditional model for a lifetime, it is possible that I may feel called in the course of my life to develop a different type of spirituality. Let us say that devotion to the Heart of Mary is highly revered in my community. Having been initiated in this type of spirituality, I have learned to live with God in the way the Blessed Virgin did. Later on, however, I may experience a special attraction to the mystery of the Holy Trinity. If they discover this, my fellow religious should not interfere. Deeply aware that the essence of religious community is to free the individual religious for their own inspiration, insofar as compatible with the essential demands of community life, they should not suggest to me that I am wrong in following my special inclination to revere the Holy Trinity because this devotion was not emphasized in the mode of spirituality through which the community initiated me into the life of the spirit.

On the other hand, the demands of community life imply that I do not discourage others, especially new members, from living our initiation model of spirituality. Some model seems to be necessary for most people if they desire to enter a life of intimacy with the Holy. I should humbly accept the fact that the average person cannot enter the spiritual life from anywhere at all, that he must approach it from some limited perspective, that he must live it in some form or shape, some limited structure, before he can discover other perspectives. Later, he may grow from perspective to perspective, never exhausting the possibilities of being intimate with the Holy.

Something similar must be said of the fields of action which the religious community makes available. Most people have to learn how to be religious participants in the culture by sharing in some cultural-religious endeavor that is already lived efficiently by other religious celibates. Hence it is probable that I shall be fulfilled by remaining in such fields of action as my community makes available for me. It is likewise possible, however, that I may grow beyond the particular types of community activity; that I, in dialogue with my community and superiors, may discover that God calls me to a quite different type of contribution still compatible with community life. In such a case the community, called to guard against the absolute and exclusive domination of religious life by any established system or work, should foster my development as a unique religious celibate. For this is the reason why I did not commit myself unconditionally and exclusively to any establishment of family, society, or diocese. I should realize, however, that whim and fancy, illusion and self-deception, may tempt me to seek a different type of occupation. Therefore, such a decision can be made safely only in full and humble obedience to superiors who in turn are obliged to honestly ask themselves one central question: How can this person best serve the unfolding of the Holy in humanity without harming the essential demands of community life?

7

Human Presence And Structure

Religious community is in tune with the fundamental significance of the religious vows. Both are meant to free the religious in a special way so that he may worship and witness for the Holy, as it unfolds itself creatively in the cultural evolvement of man and his world. The presence of the participative religious to the Holy takes the form of a free and flexible participation in the cultural trends that move his contemporaries. When I realize the exciting life of freedom for the Holy to which I am called, I ask myself, "Are there no limits to this transcendence of structures and systems? Are not participative religious and their participative religious communities also bound by structures of their own? And if structures are unavoidable even in the religious life, is there still a way in which I can transcend them so that I may live the life of worship and witness for the Holy whose call I have been so blessed to receive?"

When I think quietly about the human person, I

am bound to admit that he appears to me only as somehow structured. Reflecting, for example, on my own daily life, I realize that I could not function if I did not maintain a minimum of structure in my thought, feeling and action. It is impossible for me to be open to all revelations of reality at all times. I am aware that my body compels me to forsake any attempt at all-encompassing presence. It is clear, even when I may not want to, that I have to assent to my need for sleep. There is an initial formidable structure imposed on my personal life, one which regulates periods of activity and sleep. Even my waking hours can only be so full. I cannot at once contemplate and perform a surgical operation, pray and take a difficult examination, concentrate and totally relax. In other words, human life can be lived only in continual structuring.

Man's Finite-Infinite Polarity

Actually, it is not so strange that the development of my personality presupposes a development in structuring. As a human person I am finite and limited. Therefore, the Holy can reveal itself in me only in a finite and limited way. Only God by His very being is free from structure; only He is absolute and infinite openness to all that is at every moment. If I strive to be pure openness, to be totally free from structure, I succumb to a temptation as old as humanity itself, the desire to be like God — the deep and lasting temptation so beautifully portrayed in the story of Adam and Eve. Their story is my story. And, despite my tendency to believe the contrary, I may as a religious be more prone than other men to the temptation of Adam. Experiencing in community a greater freedom from the functional aspects of system and establishment, I may be more easily tempted than my fellowmen to strive after a liberation from all structures in myself and my community. This desire to be like God can be understood experientially if I am aware of the polarity of my own existence.

I experience in myself two needs which seem to be opposed to each other; the need for structure and the need to transcend structure. Even if I do not go to the extreme of desiring a God-like freedom and openness, I may nevertheless feel a deep urge to break through the concrete religious structures which make it possible for me to maintain my religious orientation. Another way to express this polarity within me is to say that the unfolding Holy reveals itself as a desire for the infinite, while my concrete bodily existence compels me to seek the infinite through finite structures, which in turn are surpassed by my infinite desire. I am forced to be open to infinity in a structured, finite way. Structure is the finite grasp of the infinite. My very nature compels me to live in the tension between structure and transcendence of structure.

My community, too, is caught in this eternal dilemma. Neither I nor my community can ever escape this tension which is rooted in human nature. We can only attempt to live it in a balanced, creative way by coming to terms with our need for both structure and its transcendence. If I and my community are by nature structure-bound, then we can never realize transcendence by a rejection of structure, or a despising of structure, or a foolish attempt to destroy all structure. Transcendence can only mean for us an acceptance of certain structures and yet a going beyond them, a not being confined to them.

To give a simple example: Certain people love to say the rosary. For them it is a meaningful structure opening to the Holy as manifested in the life of the Mother of the Lord. Structure is so essential for all human acts that prayer life also presupposes some structuring. When these people are truly praying, however, they transcend the structure of the rosary. They do not fixate on the necessity of counting the beads or carefully pronouncing each syllable of the Hail Mary; they rise beyond the structure of this prayer in a presence to the Holy. An analogy may be made in regard to the structures of community life. Take, for example, the structure of silence. In order to guarantee periods of privacy for each person in religious life, the community designates certain places or times during which nobody can be imposed upon unnecessarily by others. This structure of silence is not meant to be lived as an emptiness, a simple absence of words, but as the possibility for openness to the infinite.

Shared Articulated Presence

The finite-infinite polarity which I, as a religious, share with all men explains why human structures are fundamentally different from the structures which I see in nature, such as those of a tree, a flower, a rain cloud, or a rock formation. The human structure is never the structure of an object but the structure of a presence. For man is presence. As man and as human community, we are a presence to being, an openness in the density of reality, an experiential penetration into that which reveals itself to us in our surroundings. At the same time, I am not a divine, all-penetrating presence. I am limited, and therefore I must articulate my presence according to my background, my life purpose, and the demands and possibilities of the situation in which I live.

In short, I am a *structured* or *articulated* presence. Therefore, I may say that each human structure is a mode of presence to reality and that without structure no human presence is possible. Structure is the necessary condition for any human presence to any reality whatsoever. No presence is possible without articulation. To understand this I may simply consider all my actual modes of presence to the world and the modes of presence of my community in the culture. I shall discover that each real presence, whether it is praying, studying, preaching, contemplating, manual labor, aesthetic endeavors, or being together with others, has some form of structure, some articulation, some discipline, some pattern of organization.

When I consider the activities and experience which I share with my community or fellowmen, I also realize that I am never totally alone in my presence to God, man, and world. I am a *shared* articulated presence. For example, when the Holy moves me to participate in the scientific openness of man to reality, I can do so effectively only by sharing in the scientific articulation of the human presence to that which is made the object of a science by this very specific articulation. The same may be said of the aesthetic, the prayerful, the contemplative, the practical, the technical, the psychological presence to reality. Each one of these modes of openness to reality has its own structure. The knowledge, mastery and development of these effective structures of presence depend on the close cooperation of men in all periods of history. No man in isolation could discover, sustain, and creatively evolve such structures of presence.

The unusual freedom which we religious enjoy because of our liberating vows should not make us believe that we can escape this essential aspect of the human predicament. The celibate religious life as witness for the transcendent aspect of reality cannot be lived effectively without relationship to other religious who have lived a similar structure or articulation of human presence during the course of the centuries. Religious community is a concrete embodiment or incarnation of the shared articulation of this celibate-religious presence to the Holy. Such structures of community life are the fruit of the experience of generations; they have proven useful to former generations as a means of maintaining and developing religious presence. We may now be profiting from the good effects of these structures without realizing how influential they are in our life with the Holy.

Deviations of Structure

Structure and the affinity toward non-structure exist side by side in my personality and in my community. If one or the other aspect is over-stressed, we shall sooner or later experience disorder. Each extreme leads to its own type of deterioration. When I or my community neglect transcendence and confine ourselves to mere structure, we shall develop obsessive-compulsive features of thought and behavior, which mean the death of the spirit for me and my community. Such behavior may take the form of scrupulosity, or rigid legalism, and is directly opposed to the fundamental meaning of the religious life.

The celibate religious appears in the world as a witness and a sign for the transcendence of all structures, systems, and establishments. He is this living sign in two ways. First, he not only participates in the cultural endeavors of established structures and institutions, but he also goes beyond them in a seeing of the Holy which reveals itself as the value-maintaining aspect of cultural establishments. Second, he lives in an alert, spontaneous presence to the unfolding Holy as that in the culture which is a living inspiration to new experiments, opening up unexpected avenues in the unfolding of humanity. How can the participative religious be the sign of transcendence in the world if he is not able to live this transcendence at home — if the religious community does not guard it as its most precious possession?

While over-emphasis on structure leads to compulsive-obsessive disorders, a one-sided concentration on transcendence as isolated from structures likewise leads to deviations. When I or my community, in seeking to be present to the Holy, neglect structure, we shall inevitably experience a feeling of uprootedness.

Lost and forlorn, thrust out of concrete reality, we may feel schizoid and cut off from the world. The loss of our identity may be accompanied by a mounting anxiety, for identity is bound up with the experience of the concrete structures in which it is incarnated. Loss of concrete structure also results in the loss of effective activity in reality. The density of concrete thought and action evaporates into the rarified air of endless talks and imaginative flights in which we blissfully change the whole world regardless of the structure of reality. Following upon the loss of contact with reality, I may experience a terrifying emptiness, an inner confusion, and a falling to pieces of my personality. Schizoid disorders are far worse for religious and their communities than obsessive disorders. Therefore, the one-sided concentration on an isolated transcendence of all structures may be even more pernicious for the mental health of the religious community than the one-sided preoccupation with isolated structures.

Rash Destruction of Structure

It is now evident how dangerous it may be to discard a traditional structure without pondering deeply its original meaning and scope. To be sure, if we eliminate certain necessary structures, we may experience the pernicious consequences of their loss later and as a result move to restore them. Therefore, while we do not need to be overly concerned about the long range development of religious life as such, we should be concerned about the happiness and effectiveness of our own generation of religious. We have only one life to live. If I and my fellow religious cannot profit from the wisdom of former generations, we may be condemned to live a life without intimacy with the Holy. This may mean for me a lost life, perhaps a negative, bitter, confused, and resentful existence generated by unwise, impatient, and rash experimentations with patterns of religious living.

It may be recalled that a generation ago psychologists went to extremes on the issue of total permissiveness in education. With one stroke of the psychological pen, age-old structures of education were suddenly destroyed. We know now that contemporary psychology has recovered from this one-sidedness after experiencing the consequences of almost limitless permissiveness in the family. While we are grateful for the more balanced vision of psychological thought today, we feel pained when we consider the men and women who were condemned to live ineffective or neurotic lives as a result of this experiment in their families. The restoration of wisdom today cannot restore to happiness those who lost the possibility of a balanced life because of impetuous experiments with their childhood situation.

I recall another experiment from my student days. Groups of students were goaded by certain educators in certain high schools and universities to be merely negative and critical. The expectation was that the more critical and negative their attitudes, the more they would be able to correct deficient structures of the past and to establish ideal structures for the future. I remember how exciting it was to hear the critiques of these young men — the biting, sharp, brilliant way in which they dissected people and institutions. As a young man I was fascinated by their clever minds and masterful expression. What they said seemed to be true. They were geniuses in exposing the seamy side of human institutions. At the time I was too young and inexperienced to realize that they suffocated in themselves and others the ability to be joyful and grateful for the good that is done by men, no matter how marked by human limitations. Blinded by their so-called objective observation of the shortcomings in human institutions, I did not realize that they never used their brilliant minds to discover the good, the true, the beautiful, and the sublime, hidden like jewels in the dusky corners of human endeavors. Basically, they were good young men; their intentions were praiseworthy; they thought they had discovered a new avenue to joyful productive living for themselves and others. At the time I could not predict the fate which would be theirs.

Returning for a lecture series to my home country after a lapse of years, I visited these men and their families, curious about their success, their achievements, their possibly exciting lives. Men who were such masters in discovering human limitations must surely have been able to produce almost faultless works, to establish efficient organizations, and to build happy families. How shocked I was when I found embittered old men who had substituted resentment for production, who in some cases were despised by wives and children as joy killers, who brought to both professional and family life the only talent they had developed in their youth — the talent to discover imperfection and limitation. This stifling, one-sided ability had enmeshed their whole personalities and entangled itself in everything they did. They could always discover what an enterprise lacked, or what it failed to achieve. To find fault, to deride, to deprecate had destroyed their ability to admire, to wonder, to respect. Thus they suffocated the possibility for joy in their lives, for creative achievement and for all elated interest.

It may be that their sons and daughters will learn from the lost lives of their bitter fathers that they need to return to a structure of openness, not merely ascertaining the negative aspects of people and establishments but also positing the good ones, not merely perfecting the criteria to condemn but also resurrecting the ability to admire. Nonetheless, I lament a lost generation who experienced the one life they had to live as a life without fulfillment, because of a one-sided experiment in their youth. How lamentable it would be if young religious celibates of today were also condemned to an empty and joyless existence because of rash experiments which precipitately cut the tie with the great traditions of the past — traditions which have taught us that anxiety about the limitations of life can be overcome by the joy of experiencing the revelation of the sacred in all finite things.

Humanizing Structure

My presence and that of my community to reality must always be structured or articulated, though structures are never an end in themselves. They are means of being intimate with God and man. Structures are like windows that open out upon the Holy as it reveals itself in us and in our surroundings. Only when I see structures as shutters blocking out the light do they present a problem.

To say that my presence to reality as human presence must always be structured implies that these structures should manifest the dynamic or evolving movement characteristic of the truly human. What is called human is never static, motionless, or finished like a rock or a stone. To be human is to be in motion, in evolvement, in transcendence. Because this is so, the humanity of my structures can increase and deepen or diminish, decrease, and even be lost. To be structured also means to be called to a lifelong task of humanizing structure in myself and in my community by continual transcendence. Just how can I humanize the structured presence to reality which man and human community are?

The first attitude which leads to increasing humanization of structure is the attempt to view and accept structure not for its own sake, but because of its potential openness toward God and world. This insight may reveal to me that a particular structure which is most helpful for the community is less necessary for me as an individual. If this is the case, then the love and justice binding me to the community oblige me to live this structure for others even though I do not need it myself. For example, we know of saints in religious communities who were gifted at certain periods in their lives with spiritual experiences that kept them in close mystical union with God. These gifted individuals did not need the community structures of meditation and common prayer. Nevertheless, they did not exempt themselves from these exercises. They realized what harm they could do to the possibility of religious presence for their fellow religious if they encouraged them by their absence to neglect well regulated openings in the day for prayer and openness to God. The average religious needs such moments of more intensified presence to the Holy.

When I enter the community, I take upon myself the responsibility for the maintenance and development not only of the structured presence which is necessary for my own spiritual growth, but also for the growth of presence in the average member who enters with me. Growing insight and free acceptance of existing structures, and a loving acceptance of the burden of these structures, even if in an exceptional case I can live without them, increases my awareness of what they mean for the average individual.

The humanization or spiritualization of structure also demands that I try increasingly to animate the structures of my community — that I transform them from mere customs to living experiences. When I execute a custom mechanically without trying to make it meaningful for myself and others, it becomes dehumanizing and isolates me from the human presence to God and man which I should be. All inherited structures, whether in the culture or in religious life, can be dead structures for me if I do not animate them. It is my lifelong task to fill them with meaning and then to rejoice in their resurrection. But I should not expect them to come to life overnight.

Stages of Humanization

During the stage of initiation the new religious accepts and tries to assimilate gradually the structural design of religious life. The postulant or novice assumes the customs and rules of his freely chosen community and lives with them without yet understanding their manifold meanings and implications. He trusts the traditional wisdom underlying these structures and does not feel qualified to question them on the basis of his own limited experience in this new state of life. If he were to approach the customs of his community with a merely critical attitude, it is doubtful that the new religious would ever be able to experience the meaning and impact of these structures on his personality. He cannot attempt simultaneously to live new structures and evaluate them analytically. Such a critical attitude would prevent him from living these structures fully and wholeheartedly. Moreover, the criterion of his judgment would be no more than his former experiences, which relate to other life structures, or to his own reading of critical articles by authors who hopefully have experienced the advantages and disadvantages of these structures during their own long years of religious observance. However, to be initiated into these structures, persons should not become overly preoccupied with such critical literature. As we have seen, all structures are felt as an imposition, because of our desire to transcend structure. Therefore, a mere critical attitude on the part of people to be initiated into a new structural design of life will easily, if not always, find reasons to refuse them, at least interiorly. A new candidate for the religious life is not able to evaluate the structures of this life fully until he has lived them himself. Once they have become part of his flexible and gracious personality, the way is truly open for him to discover their values and limitations in a personal way. Thus the stage of acceptance is valuable *only* if it is regarded as a first stage which may then lead to greater humanization and personalization of the structures concerned.

The second phase finds the maturing person doubting the value of a rule or custom which he may have lived impersonally. This period can be the hour of grace in which he discovers that it is not necessarily the custom or rule itself which is devoid of meaning, but his own impersonal way of living this feature of community life. If he is blessed with this insight, he may attempt to experience the meaning of the structure in question so that he may live it authentically. However, if he does not experience that the way in which one lives structure is more important than the structure itself, he may strike out blindly against the rule or custom without exploring respectfully its possible value or meaning in dialogue with other members of his community.

A far worse situation may develop which would threaten the mental health and balance of the person. Unable to believe in the possibility of the meaningfulness of any structure, the religious may emotionally oppose all structuring. So doing, he restricts his basic humanity and therefore his deepest self. The result can only be an unbalanced, undisciplined, ineffective, and joyless life that cannot realistically create. In the wake of this loss of happiness and effectiveness, the religious will be overwhelmed by bitterness, jealousy and envy. He will reproach others for the failure of his life. Before long, he will angrily reject the possibility that a realistic and respectful return to structure and discipline may be one way to achieve fruitfulness and happiness in his life.

The third stage in animating the structures of my life and those of the community is the readiness, in dialogue with the community, to change structures which are obsolete. Structures which have ceased to serve our effective presence to God and man function as an arteriosclerosis which clogs up the life arteries of the community. If they are not discarded, the community will deteriorate into an isolated collectivity no longer capable of being meaningful in the world. Neglect of the timely renewal and adaptation of the structures of religious presence will sever these structures from living human openness; they will degenerate, become thing-like, frozen, and objectified. From then on, they will only hamper life and kill the spirit. Failing to transcend former structures of behavior when the situation demands such transcendence, I open myself to the deadening process of spiritual arteriosclerosis. Gradually I shall fall out of tune with my culture, unable to maintain a lively presence to the unfolding Holy in the light of the demands of my situation.

To summarize briefly, the humanization of structure implies the free acceptance of existing structures for their potential openness to God and world, and a constant readiness to transcend obsolete structures and grow toward new articulations of my presence to reality. A true openness for the Holy, as it unveils itself to us as community and as individuals, implies a relaxed readiness for change of structure when a more effective presence to the Holy as newly revealing itself in the culture demands such an alteration.

There are many aspects of human structures of presence, but two which especially call for humanization are their defensive function and their constraining character.

Defensive and Constraining Character

As a human being I may feel lost and lonely in the great universe which surrounds me and seems to absorb me. The overwhelming unknown on all sides is ready to encroach upon me. At times I experience a mounting anxiety, fear, and forlornness. To quell this anxiety, I start from the beginning of my life to structure reality. I organize my life in certain patterns, I establish a minimum of regularity, I give all things a name. The fact is that I am always structured and structuring, not only because of my necessity as a finite being to do so, but also because of my need for security. Structures of human presence are also defenses against the impact of the unknown, the untried, the irregular, and the challenging. But it is obvious that this defensiveness should not be the main source and inspiration of structuring. Our lives and communities should be structured not primarily because we are anxious, but because we are attracted by the Holy as it reveals itself in an unfolding world. Therefore, we should develop the ability to discriminate between what is inspired by the Holy Spirit and what is suggested by anxiety in the depths of our unconsciousness.

However, man and human community by their very nature cannot totally escape the defensive and protective aspects of human structuring. They are not undesirable, provided I am aware of the defensive anxiety which may arise when I have to relinquish a former structure for a new and more effective one. It is quite possible that I and the members of my community, in honest dialogue before the face of the Holy, experience that a certain rule or custom is antiquated and should be replaced by a new one or simply eliminated, and that simultaneously we experience uneasiness, displeasure, fear and apprehension in initiating the change. This uneasiness may well be the expression of the anxiety we feel when we lose a form, habit or discipline which has long functioned as a means of regulating the unknown and the irregular in our lives and surroundings.

The defensive motivation of human structures of presence should never dominate in my life or my community. Anxious defensiveness always leads to a shutting off and closing in upon myself. As a result, structures which are motivated merely by defensive anxiety become increasingly dehumanized and lose their true meaning. For the characteristic of closure is diametrically opposed to that of openness, which is precisely the essence of a human structure of presence.

It is clear that structure is necessarily constraining; it somehow regulates the flood of passion and inspiration. I say it regulates the flood for it should not cut it off. If it does, then life loses its vigor and flavor.

When I or my community experience too much constraint, a great deal of energy, initiative, and emotionality are dammed up in my personality. Too much constraint can lead to hysterical outbursts, as we know from the history of some religious communities. Of course, the problem is not solved by a futile attempt to eliminate structures completely. Helpful to some degree may be the discarding of unnecessary structures and the creation of periods of relaxation and recreation in which the members of the community feel less strongly the impact of structures on their lives.

However, the best means to diminish the feeling of constraint which all structure and discipline necessarily create is to explore my attitude toward structures. Here again, the transcendence and humanizing of structures is the best possible way to diminish the feeling of constraint. For in transcendence we are more present to the Holy toward which structure is pointing than to the structures themselves. We feel less their constraining quality and more their force to free and open up. Nevertheless, as I can never totally escape the experience of human structure, so I can never escape its accompanying constriction. Fundamentally, this experience is again that of my finiteness and my limitations.

Irrational Component

One of the unpleasant aspects of community structures which I shall always face is their unavoidable degree of irrationality. Community structures are partly irrational for me as a unique individual, and to some degree they are also irrational for every person in a community or culture. Let me first reflect on the irrationality of community structures for me as a unique person. No community structure can correspond completely with my individual needs, likes, dislikes, or even physical characteristics. To the degree that they do not suit me as an individual, they are somewhat irrational. This lack of personal adaptation of structure is due to the fact that community structures have to be adapted to a fictitious average or common person who does not exist in reality. As a result, almost no community structure exactly suits any member of the community because nobody is precisely this average individual who exists only statistically. Consider, as a simple example,the structures of chairs, tables, doorknobs, bathtubs, and light fixtures. For some they are too high or too wide, for others too low or too narrow. And then consider the many left-handed persons and those who tend to be pygmies or giants. It is clear, however, that a community or culture can only structure itself if every person is willing to bear with this unavoidable irrationality out of respect for society which could not survive as a whole without common structures. Life would be impossible for myself and others if we were constantly fighting the irrational in structure.

The above concept is even more applicable to those community structures which conflict to some degree with my psychological, temperamental, and physiological predispositions. For example, society, in order to maintain itself, has to establish certain office hours for its public institutions. It may well be that my personal physiology and psychology lead me to prefer to come to the office at night and to sleep during the day. Others may prefer to work during early morning hours. In short, I can imagine many periods of effectiveness in which various persons can labor most successfully and happily. It seems somewhat irrational that they should all conform to a certain common structure of working hours as maintained throughout society. However, the acceptance of such irrationality seems to be the only rational way to build an effective civilization. The same may be said of the structures in the religious community. It is impossible to set up times for Holy Mass, common prayers, meals, and periods of silence and recollection which are precisely the best moments for each person in the community. Therefore, it is not unusual but perfectly normal that a different time and place would be better suited to my moods, temperament, and physiological disposition. Again, it is clear that only the loving acceptance of the unavoidable irrationality in my community structure will make life possible for me and my fellow religious. It is not important that I feel a natural dislike for community structures insofar as they do not suit my personality. What I do with my dislike, how I handle it, is important. I have to work through such natural aversions by understanding that the irrational component of a community structure is unavoidable. Then perhaps I can make my acceptance of it an act of justice and love toward my fellow religious, realizing that each individual can adapt himself to common structures even if they do not suit him as well as he would like.

Here again I may take an example from my brothers and sisters who have been called to the community of marriage. They too have to adapt themselves to family structures which are common to father, mother, and children. But they can only succeed in family living when each one sacrifices to some degree his personal desires and idiosyncrasies. Or I may consider the men and women who have dedicated their lives to the regular care of the faithful. The effectiveness of their lives is dependent on compliance with the numerous structures of diocesan organizations and regulations, and compliance with the situational structures of the faithful whom they encounter daily in order to fulfill their pastoral needs.

The personal irrationality which I face in community structures is not the only component with which I have to cope. Community structures can also contain elements which are irrational for everyone, independent of our individuality. I should remember that the human being is not only rational, wise, and personal. He is also irrational, impulsive, compulsive, and prepersonal. His human expressions imply the irrational as well as the rational. This characteristic can be seen in the community structures which man has established in the course of his history. As an example, we can consider trends in fashion. A certain minimum and a certain quality of dress are undoubtedly a necessary structure in society. The concrete embodiment of this structure in fashions is partly inspired by contemporary rational demands of climate, beauty, and taste. But an irrational element is also expressed — a contagious temporary excitement which can be explained perhaps as a reaction against a former type of fashion. In other words, not every detail of fashion is rationally motivated. Interestingly enough, it is far easier for me to recognize the irrationality in fashions of former generations than in those of my own. In my daily lived experience I am not readily aware of the irrational component of my own enthusiasms, but I can diminish its impact by being aware of its presence. For example, I may be involved at present in the eager restructuring of my community. I should recognize that the new structures which I propose are perhaps partly motivated by fads and fancies which are temporary, incidental, and perhaps somewhat irrational reaction formations. I should not be disturbed by this unavoidable irrationality. Rather, awareness of this human element should make me more humble and relaxed in my proposals for change and renewal.

A real difficulty may emerge for the religious who is more aware than others of this irrational and temporal component. If it is my fate to possess such an unusual perspicacity, it may pain me to experience the enthusiasm of my fellow religious for an old or new structure which to me clearly contains an irrational element. I may dream about a period in which community structures and fashions will be impeccably rational. Such daydreaming, however, takes me out of the realm of human reality where perfectly rational structures are impossible, and perhaps in some ways inhuman, insofar as the irrational and prepersonal are necessary characteristics of man in the present phase of the human evolution. It is therefore a greater wisdom to accept structures that are accepted by an enthusiastic majority in spite of the fact that I personally experience their partial irrationality as painful.

Another source of the continuation of irrational structures can be found in the sheer weight of custom and tradition which cannot be overcome in spite of the best insight and scholarly information. I recall a learned friend who was disturbed by what he called the strange and irrational custom in our culture of sitting on chairs instead of reclining on couches while eating, conversing, or lecturing. He had collected an imposing array of data proving that the sitting position is less convenient for digestion, muscle formation, and psychological relaxation. He had proven for himself that certain past civilizations, in which people ate their meals as they reclined on divans, fared better physiologically and psychologically than ours. He waged a bitter fight to change the irrational structure of sitting in our society. He even visited famous restaurants and asked to be allowed to take his meal lying on a couch, demonstrating in this way for the renewal of a rational tradition. Recently, however, my friend has communicated to me that he has finally reached maturity. At least he is able to conform to the existing structure in spite of the fact that his superior knowledge leads him to perceive it constantly as irrational and disadvantageous. He is finally able to accept the fact that custom and tradition in the West will make it impossible for him to convince others of the necessity to abolish chairs and to replace them with beds, divans, and couches.

As a religious, I may be caught in a similar predicament in regard to certain community structures. I may be a medical doctor, a psychologist, an artist or an economist. I then have available a highly specialized knowledge which may reveal to me that certain aspects of traditional community structures are irrational from the medical, psychological, aesthetic, or economic point of view. Sometimes I may be able to convince others of this irrationality and thus promote desirable change. More often, however, I may experience that it is difficult for others who do not share my background to understand my objections, based as they are on highly specialized studies and experiences. For example, if I am an experienced psychotherapist, I cannot expect that fellow religious, who do not have the same background, will have the same sensitivity for certain dehumanizing aspects of structures. To expect this response would be highly unreasonable. What I find to be normal may seem exaggerated and far-fetched to others. Community life is only possible if the specialists in the community are able to accept serenely the fact that others cannot yet live in the truth in which they are living. I should not expect that the heavy weight of a long and serious tradition can be lifted simply by a remark on my part, the wisdom of which cannot be appreciated by others who have not made the same studies or lived through the same experiences. I can learn a lesson from the tolerance and patience manifested by the Lord toward his rather obtuse apostles and disciples.

Conservative-Progressive

In the matter of structural change, I frequently hear about those who are more conservative and those who are more progressive in relation to change. I can gain important insight by considering the necessary contributions of both types of religious. First of all, as long as I remain within the realm of religious anthropology or scientific theory, the distinction between conservative and progressive cannot apply. I cannot be a conservative or a progressive in the realm of theoretical or scientific knowledge, for in this area I am interested only in truth which can be demonstrated. Whether this truth fosters a more progressive or more conservative line of action is irrelevant to the authentic scientist. The question of favoring a more progressive or conservative stand in the renewal of structures arises only in the field of practical decisions, where I can never be completely sure what the detailed outcome will be. In other words, in matters of practical decision there is always a latitude where science or scientific theory cannot provide absolute certainty because of the imponderables involved. Here I must decide on the basis of my own experience, intuition, insight into probabilities, and natural propensities.

Weighing the traditional wisdom and value involved in the possible structural change is my wise and balanced conservative insight. Evaluating the necessity of adaptation to the present and the probable future situation is my progressive appreciation of the structure under discussion. And arriving at an educated guess as to what is best to be done in regard to concrete renewal is my final decision. A guess, no matter how intelligent, is only a guess and therefore allows leeway for a more conservative or a more progressive propensity in the person who is guessing. Some persons are by experience and temperament more open to the traditional values embodied in a new structure. Others, however, are more inclined to arrive at an educated guess under the influence of a progressive temperament. As long as both types of people are able to engage in dialogue on a high level of personal wisdom and balanced insight, as free as possible from prepersonal anger, anxiety, fear, and aggressiveness, they may reach a compromise which will lead to the wisest and most prudent decision possible in the given situation. For both types of wisdom should balance each other in order to prevent a dangerous loss of traditional wisdom or a reckless fixation on the past.

Almost invincible difficulties arise, however, when the persons concerned have not reached, or temporarily lose, this level of personal maturity, wisdom, and balance. In this case conservatism is no longer the fruit of the Spirit but the result of anxiety, insecurity, and compulsiveness on the prepersonal level; it becomes a stubborn radicalism. Similarly, progressivism, when rooted in the prepersonal realm of anger, bitterness, and traumatic experiences, becomes a blind and wild request for change without consideration of the possible values of the past. As has been stated elsewhere, the realm of the prepersonal is contagious. Groups of emotionally unbalanced religious may form around radical conservatives and wild-eyed progressives. Because the whole conflict then develops on the level of the prepersonal, compromise and consideration become impossible. If either one of these groups wins, the results are disastrous because the structure of renewal they propose is not inspired by the Spirit but by the dark depth of unconscious dehumanizing forces. It is, of course, impossible on this level to be serenely open for the light of the Holy Spirit, who cannot be heard above the roar of dark drives and passions. Therefore, the first and necessary condition for sound renewal of structure is that both conservatives and progressives attempt to live serenely on the level of the Spirit by constantly transcending those needs and drives which are not yet humanized. Only on the personal level will it be possible for both types of men to contribute their necessary insights which will bear upon the intelligent guess implied in every decision for concrete and practical renewal.

8

Personality Formation And Structure In The Religious Community

In an earlier book on religion and personality, I discussed a specific aspect of human experience which I called existential transference. A better term here may be *religious* transference. I distinguished a deifying and a demonizing transference and showed how this concept can be used to refer to certain transferential experiences which are possible in my relationships to all people, objects, and situations when I strive after them in isolation from the ground of the Holy. One of the many possible objects of such religious transference is the structure which disciplines my life and the life of my community. At certain moments when I experience deeply the goodness, truth, and beauty of human structure and discipline, I may be so elated that I identify this limited revelation of the Holy with the Holy itself. In this case, I transfer my search for the Holy to one of its limited manifestations. As a result I idolize rules, customs, and other structures as divine and absolute. But as we know, human structures are modes of openness, modes of presence, to that which is not structure itself. Structures of human presence are by their very essence roads to reality. A road is not the goal of the traveler but the means he has to traverse in order to find his destiny. It is the nature of structures of presence to be continually traversed, by-passed, and transcended. The mature religious is the person who reaches a stage in his life where he has integrated his structures of presence with his personality and life situation so well that neither he nor those around him are aware of them as structures isolated from the spontaneous movement of his personality as a whole. In and through them he moves graciously toward God, people, and world. They disappear unnoticed into the background of his serene presence to the Holy. Those who deify structures make them a matter of explicit and anxious concern. Structures become for them an end rather than an unobtrusive means through which to live reality naturally and spontaneously.

Equally harmful is the demonizing transference which sees structures of presence as absolute evils to be resisted at any cost. Paradoxically, the demonizing of personal and community structures has the same deadening effect as the idolizing transference. The idolizing of structures for structure's sake leads to a fanatical preoccupation with rule, regulation, and discipline. Such constant concern makes it impossible to rise beyond structure in our journey toward the Holy. The demonizing of all structures, on the other hand, leads to a similar, and in this case negative, preoccupation. We know that human presence is of necessity structured and that human community cannot escape form or structure. Only the divine community of the Holy Trinity is by definition unstructured because it is infinite openness — not body-bound or rooted in a local or temporal situation in a material cosmos. Consequently, when I demonize and therefore reject, resist, and despise structure and discipline, I shall be forever rebellious and dissatisfied. As long as there is human presence and human community, there will be structure and discipline. To be human is to be structured. To act as man and as human community is to submit to form, shape, and project. Continually resisting unavoidable structures means that I am necessarily fixated on them.

Thus the person who demonizes structures is as structure-bound as the person who fanatically deifies them. Both are unable in their respective adoration or damnation of structure and discipline to transcend them. I and my religious community are developing the right attitude toward structures when we are able to adapt them smoothly to the times and to bear with those structures which for specific reasons cannot yet be adapted. For beyond each structure the Holy is always waiting as a shining light. This is no excuse, of course, for refusing to improve or rebuild the structures in which we live. It only implies that none of us will live to see perfect structures of religious presence which cannot be improved. If this fact leads to a demonizing attitude toward structure and discipline, I am necessarily condemned to a bitter, complaining existence. To lose the ability to live more or less serenely with imperfect structures is to be condemned to a hell on earth. I should be on guard, therefore, against the influence of those of my unfortunate fellows who are cursed by this damnation. Encounter with them can be lethal; their bitternes and negativity may be poisonous beyond relief. Constant one-sided commerce with demonizing people will necessarily demean and depress me. On the other hand, encounter with those who carry with them the precious secret of joy and admiration, of openness in and through structures, will necessarily liberate me and enable me to see structures as roads leading to the Holy.

Upon close observation, I may find in my community three kinds of people: those who fanatically deify all community structures and are not able to go beyond them; those who angrily resist and demonize these structures and likewise cannot transcend them; and finally those who serenely experience and live the community structures as limited but necessary roads toward God and reality. These latter try peacefully to improve existing structures — ready at the same time to accept that which they cannot change immediately in spite of their desire to do so. I should respect and tolerate these three types of personalities, realizing that those who have not yet reached the stage of liberation of the third may be in a temporary phase of their development. Nevertheless, I have an obligation to myself, and to those who are placed in my care, to guard against the deadening impact of both the demonizers and the deifiers. I should expose myself as much as possible to the influence of those who with God's grace have reached the stage of relaxed equanimity toward community structures and regulations.

Predispositions Toward Structures

Aware of the necessity for structure in my personal life and the life of my community, and of the various attitudes which I may adopt toward structure, I may question whether everyone who enters religious community is predisposed to assume one or the other of these attitudes. Different groups of community members may be distinguished, each characterized by their own specific style of coming to terms with community structures. Some of my fellow religious are inclined to destroy their inner freedom by their tendency to idolize or demonize community structures. I stress *tendency* to indicate a disposition in the personality which cannot be totally eradicated but which can be dealt with as the person grows in insight and freedom. Though I may grow beyond idolizing or demonizing, the inclination to one or the other of these attitudes may always remain with me. Especially in times of stress, I may be unable to escape the experience of its attraction. Why is it that I and others in my community react to structure and discipline in such an emotional way, even though intellectually we may know better?

When I look back on my life, I may realize that I experienced the same propensity in school, in family, and in my place of employment long before I entered religious life. At moments when I am able to be thoroughly honest with myself, I realize that I would experience similar emotional difficulties in any setting where structures are unavoidable. I may infer that my fundamental emotional tendencies in regard to community structures must go back to childhood;

otherwise, they would not be so firmly entrenched in the emotional structure of my personality. This insight should generate a more understanding and forgiving attitude on my part when I discover similar tendencies in critical and complaining fellow religious who seem unable to evoke an atmosphere of joyful and relaxed creativity. When I consider the influence of childhood training on subsequent emotional dispositions toward community structures, I may again distinguish three dominant types of personality formations: the dependent receptive personality, the constrained controlling personality, and the creative, open, transcending personality.

Receptive Personality

It is likely that the over-dependent, receptive personality has developed to the utmost one of the important early experiences of human life. As a baby I had the experience of being nourished, tenderly cared for, loved and petted. This first period of my life was a paradise of pure reception. I was unable to actively structure my situation, or even to experience deeply the need for structuring. Only later was I called upon by early childhood training to replace the paradise of letting go with the reality of structuring my various bodily functions.

It may be the case with me that, because of a combination of environmental influences and certain personal predispositions, I have become fixated on the level of structureless receptivity. I may desire the warmth, sweetness, and protection of others to flow into my life without interruption. Though I have not outgrown this childish need, it may be difficult for me as an adult to recognize it as the unconscious source of my attitude toward structures. Perhaps as I grew older, I gradually devised a self-consistent rational frame to explain away my irrational feelings as being perfectly logical and in tune with reality. If this infantile disposition is thickly covered by such defensive rationality, I can only uncover it with the help of a counselor or therapist. Otherwise, it may be possible to gain some insight into it by a relaxed presence to my real feelings.

A person who is inclined to live on the level of unstructured receptivity naturally resents any suggestion that he should structure his life. Even the words *structure, discipline, restraint, rule, tradition, regulation* make him cringe. When he is faced with the variety of symbols, images, and metaphors which represent religion or religious community, he will unconsciously select those which symbolize for him the possibility of living as a warmly loved child who receives boundless care, tenderness, and understanding. Such is the image of mother church, of the community as loving family, of superiors as understanding mothers and fathers who love to sit and listen, to encourage and forgive, to be warm and sweet.

Another way to unveil my underlying disposition is to investigate my deepest responses to books, articles, sermons, and conferences. I may discover in myself a remarkable selectivity which betrays the structure of my sensitivity. I may, for example, always feel enthusiastic and fascinated when a speaker stresses the need for true encounter, love, and human warmth in our lives, when he emphasizes that we should really understand one another, bear one another's burdens, illuminate one another's lives with a ready smile and friendly encouragement. Analyzing my reaction at such moments, I may catch myself strangely elated, in a kind of ecstasy, overwhelmed by a delightful feeling that here is paradise, that the religious community, the church, the country, the whole world should be bathed in the soft glow of warm encounter, of understanding and tender love.

A similar self-analysis may teach me that the words of preacher, teacher, or writer have been unconsciously received by me in a very peculiar, one-sided fashion. I did not experience in the depths of my being that *I* should bear with others in respectful love. I only heard that *others* should bear with me. My unconscious tendency did not translate the words of the preacher in any active, creative, or mature way. On the contrary, they were translated on the level of childlike receptivity; they evoked the paradise of unstructured babyhood that deep within me I never left emotionally. This explains the strange elation, the warm delight, the soft fascination I experience when I read and hear about love, encounter, understanding, and mutual trust and care. What I really feel deep within me is something like the following: "Yes, how right he is! People, superiors, fellow religious should understand my inclinations. How wonderful life would be if my community surrounded me and bent over me as a caring, understanding mother. Yes, that would be the ideal — the religious community would care for me and nourish me tenderly and understandingly. Was that not what I really expected when I entered the warm womb of community life? And what did I find? A dreadful collection of unfeeling rules, customs, and structures. Yes, this wonderful preacher shows the way to a new world, a new religious life, in which I shall be embedded in a womb of tender understanding and warm encounter."

Honest penetration into my infantile dispositions is extremely difficult. Every step of the way will be blocked by my defensive rationalizations. The more acute my mind, the keener my intellectual development and educational background, the stronger and more logical my rationalizations will be. I can brilliantly prove, for example, that my enthusiasm for understanding, love, and encounter is inspired by self-forgetful love for the church, for humanity, and for the reformation of religious life. I may succeed so well in this rationalization and its concomitant feelings that I become a somewhat successful, though one-sided apostle for love and encounter. And in this case, if I am also a gifted teacher or speaker, I shall be sure to attract a faithful and enthralled audience who will listen with rapture to my message of love.

Such fascination will be due to the fact that many among my audience have also been fixated unconsciously on the level of unstructured receptivity. My own unconscious yearning for this paradise lost flows into my message and evokes in my listeners, who suffer from the same unconscious need, first similar yearnings, then a similar being in paradise together. During my glowing lecture on love, encounter, and understanding, they feel warm and excited; afterward they walk home in a dream; they know that life will be different from now on. They are humbly grateful to me who has filled them with a new energy and a new delight. In reality, however, I have made them regress with me to the unstructured paradise of babyhood deeply buried in their unconsciousness. This experience of the force and delight of passive receptivity has diminished in them the realistic force of coping with structures as they are. They will return to daily life debilitated, more than ever unable to face the dreary demands of the imperfect life situation which is the daily situation of man once he has left babyhood behind.

Controlling Personality

Other persons may develop a proclivity toward life and its structures which is constrictive and controlling. As we have seen, a first impressive life experience is that of unstructured boundless receptivity. Following this important experience is that of the necessity to structure life. The small child is soon trained to discipline his need fulfillment according to the demands of reality as expressed in his environment. Fundamental functions, such as eating, drinking, and elimination, have to be structured according to a prescribed regularity of space and time. Many other structures are demanded from the child: his waking and sleeping times, the division of the world into touchable and untouchable objects, such as toys and knives, or blankets and electric plugs.

The child is too small and too inexperienced to understand and appreciate the inner meaning of these structures. He learns about them chiefly under the influence of punishment and reward. He may obey in order to placate the powerful grownups around him on whom he is totally dependent. Or he may obey because he is pleased by the kindness bestowed on him when he maintains such a regular life. Or it may be that he is motivated to conform to the initial structures imposed on him because of anxiety over what will happen to him if he does not follow set precepts. It is true that even before this period of response, certain structures were imposed on him as a baby. For example, his parents did not always pick him up or nourish him when he cried for food or attention. However, in this later phase of development, he himself is called upon to initiate a certain amount of structuring. And this self-structuring affects the most fundamental functions of his little body. He experiences the necessity of ordering his life and conforming to the structures of a human community, but as yet he cannot understand the internal value and the unavoidability of structures, nor the need to transcend and humanize them.

Each new and important experience in my life compels me to assume an attitude toward that experience. Once this attitude is assumed, it is difficult, perhaps even impossible, to eradicate it totally. This does not mean that I cannot grow beyond it. It only means that such primary attitudes, deeply lived and experienced, always remain present as an inclination to experience reality again in the same way. What attitude the child will take is very dependent on the reactions of the people around him to his failure or success in these pristine attempts. It is possible, for example, that people make him feel by their extreme praise or condemnation that his conformity to cultural structures is the central issue in life; that his acceptance by people is totally dependent on his ability to structure; that outside of successful structuring there is no safety, no appreciation, or protection to be expected. To be sure, this is only one of many attitudes which the child may rightly or wrongly experience in his environment.

While this attitude may in the long run provoke a rebellion against structures, it may prompt me also to deify structure as the ultimate good in life. In the latter case, I may develop a lasting disposition of anxious preoccupation with the need for perfect conformity to all possible structuring. I may be inclined for a lifetime to adhere to rules, customs, and regulations in a blind, fanatical way which precludes openness and transcendence. It is possible, as in the previous case, to overcome this inclination, but the danger exists that it will easily recur when the life situation is threatening and insecure. In the same threatening situation in which the dependent receptive personality will regress to the stage of desiring structureless fulfillment, understanding, and tender care, the constraining controlling personality will regress to anxious conformity to structures which he lived obsessively and defensively in his early childhood. Such a personality may also be inclined to live religion in a similar way. While for the structureless, receptive person the religious life may be lived as a great pacifier or sweet mother, for the obsessive, controlling person, religion may be experienced as a constellation of saving and protecting laws, rules, and regulations. If I am thus inclined, I may be more concerned with the detailed execution of the letter of the law than with its spirit. I may idolize rules and regulations as safety devices which are true saviors in disguise. I may even go so far as to unconsciously identify the Savior Himself with idolized safeguards.

How Extremes Enter and Affect the Religious Life

Since I may have entered religious life with certain of these predispositions, I should be aware of a dual inclination, either to rebel against all structures or to idolize them indiscriminately. I should be aware that my rebellion against community structures is not so much a resistance to structures as modes of human presence, but to structures as they are perverted and deformed in light of my own one-sided perspective. Both overly receptive and overly controlling people may feel a special attraction for the religious life. The receptive personality hopes to find an overflow of generous love, understanding, and encounter. The obsessive controlling personality may enter the community in search of a perfect system of workable customs, rules, and regulations which will free him from the anxiety of making possible mistakes or faulty decisions.

Moreover, at certain periods of history, it is conceivable that either of these two types of dispositions will gain a leading influence in religious movements. For example, the obsessive compulsive attitude toward religious structures may evoke puritanical, Jansenistic, and legalistic tendencies in religious communities, or even in whole populations, when cultural conditions promote to leadership persons who are afflicted by this type of childhood deformation. Especially under adverse conditions, such as a great schism or reformation, a religious group, overwhelmed by anxiety, may seek help from persons who are inclined to idolize structure, law, and custom. In times of peril or decline, a community tends to react as individuals do. It may clutch at structures as life-savers from panic, chaos, and confusion. Certain voices may clamor to return to the rigorous rules and strictness of the "good old days" which would make life safe and secure once again.

On the other hand, there are certain historical periods when persons plagued by childhood fixation on structureless, indulgent receptivity are called upon by a religious community to lead the way. This may happen when the direction of obsessive controlling personalities has led to such an extinction of dynamism and inspiration that religious life has become lost in a web of tight rules and precepts which will kill life and love.

One extreme calls forth the other. One type of deformed personality is succeeded by the other type of personality fixated in a perverse way on another level of childhood. Unfortunately the balanced, mature, creative personality who has transcended both infantile levels — who can be respectfully present to structures while transcending them — has little or no chance of being accepted as a leader in times of turbulent change. His or her voice in its mature modulation, in its beautiful serenity and wise moderation, cannot be heard above the din of the emotional outcries of compulsive-obsessive personalities and the countercries of structureless, over-indulgent people.

Each cultural period receives the leaders which it calls for. It is therefore mostly at times when stability prevails in the population, and in the communities of their religious, that mature men and women who have reached a fullness of balance and wisdom are tolerated as leaders. These are times when there exist, on the one hand, a minimum of threats to the community and, on the other hand, a wholehearted involvement of its members in well structured tasks within the society. The relative security and peace, the relaxed engagement in absorbing assignments, has temporarily silenced the neurotic tendencies of both structureless and controlling individuals.

However, as soon as security subsides, dormant tendencies will flare up and an anxious clamor for compulsive leaders may be voiced. Later, as counter-reaction against compulsive control sets in, a demand will rise for structureless indulgent types to step forth and free the community from the obsessive domination of anxious control. This situation spells new trouble because indulgent administrators, who have not mastered the art of creative structuring and disciplining, can only weaken the community by indulging the reactive emotional demands of the members to eliminate or diminish existing structures. Their specific childhood fixation makes it impossible for such men to renew and vitalize traditional community structures or to create new ones which will be relatively lasting and in tune with the cultural situation. These leaders may easily substitute for effective discipline, a whimsical enthusiasm for temporal projects which will silence for the moment the sentimental outcry of the members for freedom, fervent action, and exciting renewal. Because such projects of renewal are not initiated on the basis of prolonged study and consideration, and are not guided by a spirit of mature discipline and self-forgetful readiness to bear the incidental tediousness inherent in every enterprise, they cannot lastingly capture the exalted imagination of a community or population whose outcry for necessary renewal is dominated by an unconscious emotional reaction against a former oppressive situation. When the novelty of the new project wears off, the self-indulging crowd will be bored, for the lasting achievement of the new demands disciplined faithfulness to its structures. Then the cry will be raised again for other exciting changes to satisfy anew a primitive need for emotional excitement hailed as life, vitality, happening, and action.

The words *life*, *dynamism*, *engagement*, *vitality* have a special connotation for people who, in reaction to over-structuring in the past, have regressed temporarily in their life situation to the level of self-indulgent presence. To them these words suggest the liveliness of the baby who, without structuring, disciplined planning or lasting commitment, reaches excitedly out toward any shining, blinking thing that evokes his curiosity and holds onto it until he is bored. To be sure, persons with such childish reactions cannot know that they are emotionally disposed in this way. The problem is more psychological than moral. On the level of rationality, they may have brilliant explanations of why they live in constant change. Even outsiders may be moved by their highly charged exaltation, their grandiose ideas, fascinating plans, and striking proposals for the paradise to come, so that they too are magnetized by the strong emotional currents which touch similar powerful tendencies in their own unconscious. Since they are not trained in psychology, they are usually unable to identify the destructive negative forces — the undisciplined dark drives — which are masked as shining religious inspirations. Often the only way open to the untrained observer is to analyze quietly and constantly the quality of concrete effectiveness and the quantity of worthwhile production of the people who write and speak so splendidly about the rebuilding of community. If there is a wide gap between the flow of ideas, projects, and new beginnings, and the observable lasting realizations, the observer can suspect that unconscious fantasy life has taken over as a substitute for the quiet, persistent conquest of reality in the daily task.

Only indulgent leaders are tolerated by people who live in the mood of the emotional excitement just described. Usually the very predispositions of such leaders, who may in other respects be kind and holy men or women, may make it emotionally impossible for them to recognize the somewhat hysterical tendencies which have arisen in the community to the diminishment of realistic, consistent productivity. Even if this insight would strike the indulgent leader in a moment of clarity, it would be almost impossible for him to dare to remedy the situation. For such action would presuppose sudden growth beyond his specific childhood fixation into full maturity, which would free him not only from his over-indulgent attitude toward life and community but also from his own need to be accepted by all. This latter need would make it impossible for him to take an heroic stand against the mass hysteria around him. He would know and fear the violent outcry against him which would result.

Here again I should be careful not to judge the morality of such leaders who may not have sought their positions, but who simply were carried to the top on the waves of hysterical demands of the crowd who, in over-reaction to control, clamored for indulgence. I should not condemn, especially because one of the main symptoms of the childhood fixation of the over-indulgent leader is an overriding need to be liked, to be loved, to be popular, to be a "regular guy" accepted by everyone. In other words, there is a childish inability in the indulgent leader to distance himself, to tolerate unpopularity, to live a mature life of self-reliance not dependent on the vulgar assent of the crowd. It requires maturity to imitate Christ who could bear to be condemned by His own people, betrayed by one of His own disciples, and left alone by His friends when He did not indulge them with dreams of grandeur and earthly renewal. Because of his inability to distance himself from popular assent, the indulgent leader is unable to restore his community to the quiet dignity of disciplined engagement. He could not bear the unpopularity and abuse which would inevitably be heaped upon him when, by his very action, he would unavoidably arouse neurotic anxieties in those who trusted him in the first place. Resistance might even become so massive that he could not continue as a leader.

Such periods of emotional reaction as those described above are usually stronger than the mature individuals who could point the way. It may well be that humanity and religion simply have to bear with inferior leadership in times of reaction against compulsive or indulgent structures of the past. It is better for the majority of people to have inferior leaders than no leaders. In a sense, it may be a waste for mature creative personalities to lose energy in an effort toward leadership which may fail in times of hysteria. Here again it is important that a religious community be structured in such a way that it does not easily deteriorate into a crowd, a collectivity, or a mediocre togetherness. For such a commonality easily becomes the victim of prevailing unconscious moods and cannot find in its own ranks individuals who can represent and symbolize the transcendent individuality which resists the domination of prepersonal needs and fears.

Creative Personality

Up until now we have discussed only the structureless indulgent personality and the over-structuring compulsive personality. We have seen how they act in regard to community structures and in relation to the administrative or spiritual leadership to which they may be called in certain historical periods. While analyzing their emotional attitudes toward community structures, we alluded to a third type of personality — the creative, open, transcendent person who has overcome his fixations on the two levels of childhood already described. This is the person who has the most effective and serene attitude toward community structures. If the Holy has graced me with this maturity, I am able to bear patiently with superfluous structures which I cannot change and still live wholeheartedly the structures which are in tune with the contemporary situation. At the same time, I transcend all these structures by constantly going beyond them in a presence to the Holy. I experience in myself a special sensitivity for the appeal to the Holy as unfolding in mankind and in my culture which helps me to adapt to existing structures or to create new ones when the situation demands.

This grace of presence, this serene, relaxed, and efficient attitude toward community structures, can be maintained if I keep my life attuned to the Holy. Deifying or demonizing of structures always implies that in some way I experience them as absolute and ultimate. To perceive any structure as absolute good or evil is impossible the moment that I am absorbed in the Holy as my absolute ground and last meaning. The more I grow in intimacy with the Holy, the less I am liable to be seduced by an excessive or absolute concern with structures. When I discover in certain periods of my life that I am more than usually irritated by structures in my community, these are the times to question myself about my prayer life, my recollection, my hours of waiting silence, my spirit of intimacy with the Lord. When these diminish, the pressure of structures increases. When these flower, structures are light things to bear for Him who allows them to be in my life situation.

As we have seen, respectful mutual distance, a letting-be of one another in privacy, is the hallmark of a mature religious community. Mature religious, who have reached in their lives the stage of creative, disciplined openness toward reality, can remain quietly effective and productive within their own respected privacy. In spite of the tumult of exaggerated claims and counter-claims, of excited community gossip; in spite of the turmoil and excessive rigidity or over-indulgence that shakes others, they can remain recollected and in tune with the Holy, waiting for the grace that will calm the minds and hearts of God's people in His own good time. They can live their lives graciously, in kind, patient understanding of the emotional excitement and upheaval around them, and at the same time reserve their energy for the disciplined production of lasting work in the service of the Holy, Who strengthens and guides their creative flow.

In thus being themselves, the mature religious may constitute within the community a calming influence which may point the way to true maturity and renewal in serene self-discipline. When the community or population regains balance and equanimity, they will always be there as people one can turn to when a lessening of anxiety and turmoil opens the way to mature acceptance of structure and discipline. And if they should not live to see the return of balance, their lives are still not lost because their example, and in some cases what they have said or written, may be discovered in the future as guiding lights for a new period.

9

Encounter And Its Distortion In Community Life

Following our discussion of the meaning and structure of the religious community, we may now consider the mode of encounter which should prevail in community as lived by participative religious. Before we attempt to discover this particular mode of encounter, however, we should inquire about the meaning of encounter in general and about its various constituents.

Modes of Human Encounter

Human encounter can be lived in many modes, equally human, equally respectful, yet different in the sense that each stresses one of the essential aspects of encounter as primary, making its other aspects less prevalent and more implicit. Human encounter can exist between husband and wife, employer and employee, salesman and buyer, therapist and client, teammates, intimate friends, and people collaborating in common projects. Social life contains such an inexhaustible richness of relationships that this list could be expanded indefinitely. Reflection on daily experience reveals, moreover, a multiplicity of shades and nuances in the modes of human encounter. When I encounter my fellowmen in various social fields, structures, and settings, I experience a different style of encounter each time. A husband does not meet his wife in the same way that he meets the waitress in his favorite restaurant, even if he regards her with respect and appreciation. An employer meets his employees in another mode than he would meet his friends for a hunting trip. Likewise, the profile of encounter which is typical of religious life differs from that of any of the above examples.

How can I explain this variety of modes of meeting others, even when my encounter in these various situations is equally personal, honest, loving, and respectful? I may find an answer in light of one of the fundamental working hypotheses of anthropological psychology, namely, that being man is being in a situation. In other words, I cannot indicate any human mode of life without at the same time indicating how the situation enters into the very structure in which this mode is lived. This hypothesis implies that I can never speak about a specific human encounter without taking into account its situation. A true meeting of two persons implies respectful obedience both to the situation that we share and to the situation that belongs to the other as his personal life sphere and unique destiny. For example, a respectful relationship between employers and employees takes into account that both are called to produce the best possible goods to enhance the living conditions of the consumer. Moreover, their situation demands that both strive efficiently for profits which will benefit the company and thus assure increasingly higher standards of living for employers, employees, shareholders, and their families. Authentic encounter between employers and employees thus implies that neither will thwart the inner logic of this situation by letting only personal elements in their encounter prevail over the more functional. If the personal were to prevail absolutely, the structures of production would be weakened, the specific encounter situation would lose its meaning, and the enterprise would finally destroy itself.

For example, employees might lose hours on the job telling their bosses about countless personal problems upsetting them. Or employers might feel obliged to find out how their employees feel, encouraging them to express their deepest concerns. Such a company would soon be transformed into an amateur therapy center doomed to failure because it would still be competing with other companies producing marketable goods, not expendable tears. On the other hand, the personal element should not be totally absent in the contact between company men. Otherwise, no encounter would be possible, for some degree of personal presence is one of the necessary constituents of all authentic encounter. In the case of the productive company, however, the functional aspect comes into the foreground; the personal remains present, but in the background where it permeates the functional interaction, making it respectful and human but not interfering with the primary purpose of the industrial enterprise.

Some opposite characteristics are evident in another situation of encounter: the meeting of two young people ardently in love. Even though the personal aspect of romance prevails, the functional is not totally absent. The dominance of the personal here is in accord with the situation, quite different from a meeting between employer and employee. The purpose of an engagement is growth in intimacy so that the Holy may unfold itself in a new family unit. The very aim of an intimate love situation would be distorted if the engaged couple were merely to meet functionally, discussing only clever computations of the cost of the furniture and cooking utensils for the efficient organization of their future home. On the other hand, if the functional were totally absent, their loving encounter would be untrue and inhuman. The couple will naturally conform to certain customary signs of affection established by their culture, such as kissing in Western populations or nose-rubbing among Eskimos. The lovers do not institute these functional signs of mutual tenderness; they adopt them, not necessarily as the primary element in their encounter, but as a significant, pleasant, unavoidable background for the expression of personal love. Perhaps after years of marriage, the functional will still prevail even in those moments when the husband leaves his wife in the morning and returns in the evening. Now the kiss may no longer be prevailingly an expression of personal love but a functional ceremony the married couple feels obliged to repeat morning and evening. On the other hand, if the functional takes over completely, the encounter between married people is no longer what it should be ideally.

In my meeting with fellow religious, it is also helpful to keep in mind the difference between a friendship which may emerge as a gift in my life and the average relationship which exists between religious. It is possible that by a happy coincidence I may meet in my community a person who manifests so unusual an affinity with my personality that a friendship emerges, but religious are no exception to the general population in which many people live a lifetime without experiencing the gift of finding a true friend. The majority of people enjoy the fellowship of dependable acquaintances and reliable comrades, but few are so blessed to find a person of such rare affinity that a deep and lasting friendship develops. When this happens, the friendship encounter, like the employer-employee relationship or any other, will be of a different nature than the usual encounter between religious. At the moment, our aim is to discuss the essence of the latter, without risking idealization by ascribing to it elements which are essential for intimate friendship or married love.

Fundamental Structure of Encounter

Many approaches may lead to an understanding of my own experience of human encounter, but one which may prove immediately helpful is to dwell for a moment on the word *encounter* itself. I share with all humanity an original presence to the fundamental phenomenon of human encounter. The word was coined to express this common experience. The term *encounter* is made up of two different words: *en* and *counter*. In Old French, I discover that the word underlying the English expression is *encontre*, which also can be split up into separate words: *en* and *contre*. Going back to the Latin which influenced the French, I find that the *en* is related to the Latin *in* and refers to the experience of being in, being with, being identified with, being at one with: in short, the experience of *in-being*. On the other hand, the French *contre* and the English *counter* are related to the Latin *contra* which has the opposite meaning of *in-being*. For *contra* means against, being opposed, being different, not being identified with. It is interesting to note that the word *encounter* was initially used to express a hostile meeting with enemy troops in battle.

Critically, of course, such word analysis does not of itself assure that I shall understand more clearly the experience of encounter, which may have been related to the word in an accidental way. But word analysis is a mental play which opens up possible avenues of insight into the fundamental structure of one of my experiences. If it does not bring me into touch with the experience, I shall discard this approach and seek others. The important thing is to discover what encounter means in relation to my religious life.

True encounter seems to be a polarity of in-being and counter-being: both experiences seem to be necessary in a real encounter between *persons*. For the fact that we meet *as persons* and not as things, or objectified people, is the ground out of which the *in* and *counter* experience emerges. To be a person means to be a unique, creative, and creating expression of the unfolding Holy as no thing, rock, stone, or animal can ever be. To be a person means that at the core of my being I am a mystery for myself and for others, known only to the Holy, Who increasingly reveals me to myself when I am able to be silent before Him. To be a person means that both I and the other are, in the deepest dimension of our existence, unique orientations in the evolvement of humanity, so unique that it will be impossible ever to communicate to each other exhaustively and perfectly what we fundamentally are.

That I and my fellow religious are persons therefore means that somewhere in each of us is a region where no understanding is possible. To force understanding in that last sacred realm of the personality leads to misunderstanding. My attitude toward this inner sanctuary should be one of awe, of respectful withholding, and of holy fear to desacralize or offend. No matter how profoundly I can identify with most aspects of the personality of my fellow religious, I can never identify with this radical center of his life where in a personal, unique way he is rooted in the Holy and flows forth from it as a new and original presence among men. Any vain attempt at total and ultimate identification will lead to self-deception and to irreverent betrayal of our mutual uniqueness.

This unique expression of the Holy in the personality of my fellow religious and in myself is the source of the counter-experience, which is one essential part of community encounter. Encounter is only possible to the degree that I discover the other religious as not being me. Similarly, I am revealed to myself as not being the other. Mature religious experience one another in the community as unique, and therefore, sometimes contrary centers of insight and decision. Only when we are sure that we respect one another in our uniqueness — that we shall not impose upon one another, or seduce one another to be unfaithful to the personal call of the Holy — can we feel free to experience the in-being of encounter. So long as we are unsure of this mutual respect for what we are, we shall not be able to relate to one another freely and to merge with the community without anxiety. All we can hope to achieve is a pseudo-encounter, which is nothing more than a vain attempt leading to the disappearance of one person into the other or into a faceless collectivity. Experience of the latter situation may instill distrust of all attempts toward encounter in the future. Ordinarily, deep-seated fears about personal relationships go back to unfortunate childhood experiences in which parents, incapable of respectfully encountering their children, overwhelmed them with their personalities, sometimes even in the name of religion. So long as such victims of parental disrespect do not find a person who respects them deeply in the intimacy of encounter, and who never tries to abuse their need for in-being in order to indoctrinate them into his own way of life, they will not be able to grow toward respectful encounter themselves.

Paradoxically, religious who unconsciously fear encounter because of indignities suffered from parents are often most vulnerable for those fellow religious and spiritual directors who, under pressure of their own unconscious needs for security and adulation, likewise try to overwhelm them. In such religious the fear to encounter others leads to a repression of their increasing need for in-being, intimacy, fellowship, and human love. As a result, this need grows so strong that at any moment it can break through and overpower them. As the experienced therapist, novice-master, or seminary director well knows, such a person may even subtly invite the other to overpower him with his insights, moods, advice and loving care. Therefore, one of the aims of the preparation for the religious life is to help candidates grow to encounter superiors and fellow religious in freedom, respect, relaxation, and joyful self-reliance.

Relaxed respect for the other is impossible without quiet self-respect for oneself as a unique manifestation of the Holy. A problem may arise in some religious communities because certain individuals who have not achieved the art of respectful encounter with their fellowmen nevertheless feel unconsciously attracted to religious life. Somehow they imagine religious life to be a paradise for the fearful and overdependent, who can blend indiscriminately with the community and surrender personal responsibility. If this personality deformation is deep-seated, the person cannot be admitted to participative religious life. He would betray its essential orientation, which is to send men and women forth into the world as self-reliant participants in the culture, able to encounter people in quiet dignity and self-respect. Moreover, such a person cannot contribute to the essential inner task of the community, which is to foster one another as unique, independent witnesses for the Lord. Instead, he would be a hindrance to others with his constant demands for attention, his overdependency on fellow religious and superiors, his need to be socially entertained, and his unconscious desire to cling like a parasite to those who can outline every detail of life and action for him.

Emotional Inversion of Community

When many overly dependent people belong to the same participative religious community, they may unconsciously diminish or destroy its essential calling to cultural participation by fostering an emotional inversion of community life. Thus the affective forces of the community are increasingly withdrawn from the individual fields of cultural and social engagement in the world and invested in mutual relationships and social togetherness within the community. Such emotional inversion can be far worse than the functional and political introversion described in Chapter Five as destructive of the essential orientation of participative religious life. The emotional has a far greater hold over our personality than the functional and political. Soon the emotionality and affectivity of the religious may be completely absorbed in unconscious competition for the appreciation of superiors or fellow religious. This leads to petty jealousies, anxious preoccupations and eager gossip which leave the religious too emotionally exhausted to be fully present in his field of cultural or social engagement. Such a situation may even lead to psychosomatic symptoms in persons who feel they have lost the unconscious battle for love and attention in an inverted religious community. Psychosomatic suffering obviously makes it difficult for the religious to be totally and wholesomely available for their primary task in the world. Finally, a community plagued by emotional inversion is a breeding ground for emotional disorders which make the religious a caricature of the self-reliant, relaxed, and joyful witness for the Holy which he is called to be.

Persons stricken by emotional need, who strive to

set the community on the road of emotional inversion, may not know on the conscious level what force is driving them. On the level of reason, emotional needs are translated into an idealistic idiom that exalts the religious life. Psychologically, these victims are unable to see that theirs is a deeply frustrated, unconscious emotional need which did not find fulfillment in childhood. They have entered religious life expecting to find the fullness of love and care which they have thus far missed. If I am such a religious, I am still a little child psychologically. I am not self-reliant but driven by the desire that others care for me completely. Therefore, I am deeply disappointed when I discover that the religious community is not the protective mother I dreamed it would be. The battle cry for renewal becomes for me the demand to remodel community on the criterion that it should manifest merely a loving togetherness which takes us out of the cold world and bestows upon us an abundance of maternal love and solicitude.

Distortion by Seduction

One of the greatest distortions of true encounter is seduction masked as encounter. In seduction, I try to circumvent the *I* of my fellow religious as a unique center of insight and decision by playing upon his prepersonal needs which are not yet illuminated by the center of his being where the Holy reigns as increasing Light. This dark realm of unelucidated needs, drives, and passions is less permeated by the light of insight in childhood than in later periods of life. Therefore, as a child I was especially vulnerable for parental seduction, masked as love and care. One reason for the contemporary prevalence of seduction as a veiled attack on the integrity of the other is the widespread disapproval of open attack. Many parents, friends, acquaintances, clergymen, administrators, lovers, and marriage partners have assimilated this contemporary repulsion for openly violent attempts to subdue the other. As a result, violence has gone underground and manifests itself in subtle, seductive words and gestures, in soft appeals for love, understanding, and "really being with me," in touching manifestations of "how much I love you and care for you, so much in fact that I would do anything for you." What child has a chance to escape such sweet violence without feeling guilty, contemptuous, and unholy because of his blunt refusal of parental love and care which he so badly needs in any case? When parents engage in the sweet violence of seduction, the child's chances to grow to self-reliant, fearless encounter are slim indeed. He may be worse off than the child exposed to open violence, since this is far easier to recognize and may in a stronger child provoke a healthy rebellion which can save the sanctuary of his inner personality.

In contemporary public life, veiled violence has assumed the form of subtle play on various prepersonal needs and fears which have been fostered by society itself, such as an anxious need for popularity, for being in with the crowd, for status, prestige, and promotion, for possessions as symbols of success. Somehow modern life has instilled in men overpowering fears in regard to these matters. Pressed by anxiety, many are willing to sell their birthright, the uniqueness of their personality, for a pseudo-encounter which promises fulfillment of needs and a quieting of fears which are gnawing away at the innermost realms of their personal lives. Therefore, seduction today is usually dressed in explicit or implicit promises of ascendance in power, status and popularity if only one will surrender his deepest self to the desires, evaluations, and projects of others. These others are not only individuals but also groups of people, of potential voters, of employees, academicians, or students, who attempt to seduce one another and their authorities by promising popularity, adulation, and acceptance if only one will live in cheap pseudo-encounter with others or court one or the other kind of crowd.

Contemporary man lives in a situation of massive seduction. Frequently born and reared in a seductive family, he grows up only to find himself in a school where classmates and friends seduce him to surrender his deepest self in exchange for their acceptance. Afterwards, he is inserted in a society that constantly attempts to seduce him to do things which he really does not want to do, but in which he nevertheless engages because he cannot resist the needs and fears which lurk below his real self, and which are constantly increased and abused by his seductive life situation. Living only the in-being of encounter and not the counter-experience of his unique selfhood and the selfhood of others, he is doomed to live an existence regulated solely by the crowd. He shuns all that reminds him of the demands of the inner person or threatens the walls of repression built so carefully around the appeals of his deepest self by a masterful and massive forgetfulness.

One great peril to the integrity of the religious life lies in seduction dressed in the language of the spirit. Perhaps I can best express this type of seduction in the sentence: To be liked is to be charitable; to be disliked is to be uncharitable. This is a false statement. If I adhere to it, I can indulge my need for security, popularity, and adulation by giving in to the emotional needs of the people around me and simultaneously quieting my conscience because their love and admiration seem to prove how charitable I am. Is it not true that everyone in the community, and even outside the community, appreciates how wonderful, how approachable, how understanding I am? Father is truly an easy going, regular guy! It would be impossible to have an argument with him. Sister is so sweet, so humble, so self-effacing. She fits in perfectly with every situation and satisfies even the most discontented people inside and outside the community! Unfortunately, it is not true that my popularity proves my charity or that its absence proves the opposite. By this standard, the most disliked man of history, Christ the Lord, would be a failure. The same may be said of many saints. The real story of their lives may have been romanticized by biographers who, because of their own unconsicous needs and fears, created the image of a saint beloved by all. The true story is that a saintly man or woman inspired by true charity, who appeals to the best in all, is usually not loved by all.

Consequently, I can be reasonably sure that I am deceiving myself when I unconsciously believe that my being universally liked is proof of my charitableness. A closer view may reveal my popularity to be a proof of my lack of charity, of my self-centered abuse of the lower needs of others so that I may bask in their adulation, or at least win their approval. True love would enable me to transcend my need for acceptance. Authentic charity would render me an ally of the unfolding Holy in the core of their being — of the Spirit in the heart of their existence — an ally against the confused and confusing fantasies disabling their lives. Only true charity enables me to cut mercilessly through sentimental needs and to bear with the emotional rage, the aggressiveness, and the spiteful resentment I encounter when I do not cater to the other's distorted fantasies about what life should be like.

The same is true for the crowd as well as for individual persons. Authentic charity can be at times the shortest route to universal dislike. Our Lord was the very incarnation of God's authentic love among men. If He had surrendered to the fantasies of His people and promised them an earthly kingdom of power and glory, He would have become a popular, beloved king on earth. But He loved His followers too authentically to allow them to vegetate in their fantasy and appealed instead to their highest spiritual possibility of becoming. The true lover desires what is best for the beloved even though it may cost him popularity. The Lord is the prototype of every religious who desires to grow toward authentic encounter with his fellow religious and with people in his field of cultural activity.

Community Encounter and World Encounter

When I enter community I am not free from the influences of this society which craves false encounter.

To see how this influence may poison my encounter not only in community but also in the world, I should like to dwell on the problem of encounter I shall meet when engaged with cultural partners in a common task. The problems I incur as a religious are more often than not compounded by those of my cultural partners in the world. An insight into the relationships between the religious, his cultural partners, and the people entrusted to his care may reveal to us the false aspects of encounter we should recoginze and purify in and through community life.

When my cultural partner comes to me, a religious coworker, nurse, or teacher, to discuss his problems, he may not wish to grow to the wisdom of true encounter or to free a self shackled by the prepersonal needs and fears which social systems and establishments evoke in him. He is not consciously motivated by a desire to be elevated or liberated for true presence to reality. His complaints are more prosaic. He seldom realizes that he suffers from failed encounter, constant seduction, and imprisonment by his search for popularity and status. On the contrary, he complains about vague feelings of dissatisfaction. He does not know what is wrong with his family, the institution where he is employed, his church, or the society to which he belongs. Unfortunately, his discontent is not a wholesome, invigorating orientation toward change in areas where either alone or with others he could effect a change. It is a kind of disease that has struck the core of his being in a destructively negative way. He can no longer transcend the structures of system and establishment. They have compressed his vision to the point where he has completely lost his inner freedom. What should remain peripheral has become central, and what should be a partial concern has become total. The very possibility of a serene presence to the Holy as the center of his life has been lost. He has substituted peripheral identity for his own radical identity. This false and negative identity saps the strength of the true and positive self of this afflicted personality. The more he loses ground, the more he is compelled to build up his negative external self. He cannot bear to face the growing emptiness within himself. The applause and adulation of those who suffer from the same disease affirm his negativity, which he now regards as a sign of exceptional strength, of gifted and charismatic vision. In moments of despair, when the hollowness of his life seeps into his consciousness, he may be attracted by the peace and relaxed joyfulness of his cultural partners who are celibate religious sisters, priests, or brothers. He may confide in me, his fellow administrator, scholar, teacher, or nurse. Before long, the poison of his resentment will seep into his words and stories. Unable to experience true encounter, he will subtly beg my surrender to his universe of sordid perception. He will insist that I accept his negative perspective above any other. He will declare that I am not his true friend or a true friend of God if I do not see things as black as they are in this hopeless institution where one cannot possibly work, teach, or properly care for the sick.

How useless I would be as a witness for the presence of the Holy in and beyond structure and limitation, if I too lived a false identity preoccupied mainly with the negative aspects of reality. In this case, I could not be a source of light for my cultural partner; I could only add fuel to the fire of negativity that consumes his life. His world of cynical disapproval and cancerous discord with his surroundings would find a ready disciple in me. Not having a real personality of my own, I would fuse blindly with his emotional universe and become a disgrace to the Holy instead of a source of grace in a wounded society.

Attitude of True Encounter

Maintaining, on the contrary, an attitude of true encounter is not easy. I shall initially, and perhaps lastingly, invite repeated resistance among the discontents who come to me for relief of their symptoms without desiring to be relieved of their source: the need for negative identity. True encounter implies for both of us the counter-experience which in turn evokes the awareness of selfhood, personal responsibility, and the beautiful but painful plight of the man who assumes responsibility for his own peace instead of expecting it from his environment. No wonder that the person who has nestled snugly for a lifetime in the womb of a seductively approving society cannot feel excitement at the prospect of assuming responsibility for his own peace and presence to the Holy. It is true that he disapproves of society, but the deepest ground of his disapproval is that society no longer approves of him. His situation is unbearable precisely because he has never been able to discover his true identity as rooted in the Holy. Rather, he identified himself with acceptance and approval by others; afterward losing his popularity, he could identify himself only in a negative way by rejecting society and identifying with a group who idolized him because of their own similar disease.

Unable to bear the tension of in-being and counter-being in fruitful dialogue with others, he invites relationships which are *only* in-being or counter-being. When he meets people who do not identify with his emotional negative impositions, he feels only the counter-experience and adopts an attitude of rejection and opposition in no way moderated or illuminated by the many possible experiences of in-being which he can share with others in the same situation. If, on the other hand, a person identifies with his outlook, or even if he only imagines it, he will experience and demand total in-being, unable to tolerate the possibility that the other's perception and appreciation of reality is in any way different from his own.

This sickness can be healed by the gift of true encounter which I, as a religious witness for the dignity of the person, may be able to initiate. Though this experience may evoke an unconscious continual battle between us, his true self may emerge at the moment he experiences that authentic encounter is unspeakably more satisfying than its artificial substitutes: faceless fusion and blind blending with a collectivity, or absolute condemnation and rejection of anyone who does not identify with his life orientation. No intellectual explanation of this experiential truth can be stronger than the overwhelming feeling of false security or negative identity which he has enjoyed up to now. Strong experiences like these can only be overcome by another experience equally strong or stronger, never by an abstract argument. True encounter with a religious could be one of the situations which may grant the modern man this counter-experience of his uniqueness and his responsibility for his own peace and presence to the Holy. Such encounter could be the blessed beginning of a blossoming forth of his personal life. Especially when it is accompanied by a gradual decrease of pervading dissatisfaction with life, it may become clear to him that an increase in serenity and happiness accompanies the experience of true encounter.

True encounter in community implies the relaxed and courageous experience that in many dimensions we are not the same; that we should be different; and that the belief that we can completely understand one another is a pleasant deception which protects us from the painful labor of growing up and facing reality. If I cannot tolerate the creative tension of true encounter in the community, I may fall into relationships of pseudo-encounter against which I have to witness when I am on my own as a self-reliant man or woman in the world. Identifying with fellow religious who blindly agree with all that I am or think, or with whom I fuse and blend indiscriminately, is one such pseudo-encounter — a prepersonal form of sentimental in-being. The total rejection of fellow religious who manifest maturely that they disagree with me, or cannot understand and accept all that I am, may lead to another one-sided attitude of encounter, namely, the exclusive fostering of the aspect of counter-being leading to rejection and negativity. In this case, I may become a source of division within my community. By associating exclusively with fellow religious who feel the same as I do, I may organize tightly knit groups of cohorts who maintain against others a closed attitude of rejection and condemnation.

As I grow to maturity in my community, however, I shall lose my childish hunger for overdependent emotional in-being, warm acceptance, and popularity. If necessary, I can live my own life serenely in respectful appreciation of others, even if they do not respect me nor foster my unique development as a witness for the Holy. When the grace of God grants me this equanimity, I am ready to really begin my task in the world as a self-reliant, mature participant in the great drama of human culture.

10

Dimensions Of Community Encounter

Prepersonal Likes and Dislikes

Encounter entails not only the fundamental *in* and *counter* dimension but also a *personal* and *prepersonal* dimension. In true encounter it is the personal dimension which assimilates, illuminates, and transforms the prepersonal level of togetherness. While the needs, anxieties, passions, and predispositions of my personality should not be repressed, they should be permeated by my personal commitments and ideals. Encounter is not truly encounter if it is based on a denial of the prepersonal; desire, emotion, and passion on this level give color and warmth to my encounter. Neither, however, are blind need and desire, unelucidated by the personal, encounter in the human sense.

Prepersonal likes and dislikes are related to my personal history, family background, education, and temperament; they are activated when I meet persons who sometimes by their very appearance elicit a spontaneous sympathy or antipathy in me. In a community of participative religious who serve in a variety of cultural dimensions and professions, there is bound to be a diversity of temperaments, characters, talents, and backgrounds. This implies a considerable variation of profiles of impulsive likes and dislikes. Within the same community we may find musicians and bursars, sculptors and cooks, scholars and manual laborers, philosophers and technicians, composers and pastoral counselors, poets and lawyers. Hence, in the active religious community certain individual religious celibates may not spontaneously experience a liking for each other on the prepersonal level.

In this case, true encounter can occur only when I transcend prepersonal dislike by growing in respect for the other in a dialectical way. This means that I do not repress my awareness of dislike for the other. I converse with it and admit my own spontaneous antipathy. But I do not stop here. I go on to the point where I can *will* the salvation of the other and his unique witnessing for the Holy in spite of the fact that I cannot feel at ease with him and his style of thought and action. My personal center of freedom and insight — illuminated by Grace and Revelation — will tell me in what deeper sense I can experience in-being even with one whom I impulsively dislike. I believe that we are one in God's love for us. We share His redemption and His call to witness for the Holy in the culture. Therefore, I am willing to respect my fellow religious and to safeguard the necessary conditions for his free and private unfolding. I say respect, for unfortunately the word *love* has been burdened with other meanings which do not pertain to its essence. For some, love is confused with liking and disliking. But I can dislike a person intensely and yet love him so deeply that I always show him the respect which he deserves as a human being and a person called by Christ. Similarly, I can have a profound liking for a person and not love him at all. When I am invited to do something concretely for him, I may not be willing to do so because I am lacking in love.

When I experience a person as a possible fulfillment of my needs, desires, fantasies, and ambitions, I like him spontaneously. Likes and dislikes are bound up with self-centered expectations. Indeed, all liking implies a reference to self, a certain self-centeredness. My impulsive liking is rooted in my perception or expectation of what a person can be for me. To be sure, it is far from strange that I spontaneously like what pleases me and corresponds to my needs and self-interests. Liking is harmful only if it becomes the ultimate criterion of my relationship with others — if it dominates my relationships to the exclusion of concern for the other as other. In this case, liking displaces loving and makes true love impossible. All that I really do is imitate the words and actions of love in order to make the other subservient to my need for affection, protection, and affirmation.

In love, I am responsive to the other as other, to what he is beyond the fulfillment of my needs. I not only love him for what he can mean to me, but for what he is in himself — a unique call of the Holy for his own self-perfection. It is precisely this aspect which turns liking into loving and which must prevail if love is to be salvaged from the onslaught of needs and fears which dominate the life of likes and dislikes. At times, liking must be sacrificed in order that my love may be saved. The truer my love, the more unselfish it can be if the situation demands forgetfulness of self. To like and to love may go together, but if my love is authentic, I shall be ready to sacrifice my liking out of love. For example, I may like a counselee, a young friend, a novice, or a student for his childlike dependency on me. It fulfills my need to be needed by him. It appeals to me to feel wise, important, and helpful. But it is my true love for him as a unique call of the Holy which enables me to sacrifice my liking for his attractive, childlike surrender. I realize that my attraction for his dependency and his adulation of me tend to keep him dependent and immature. True love for him inspires me to foster his selfhood, personal responsibility, and independent judgment. My love for him is stronger than my liking and enables me to bear with his temporarily unwise utterances and incidental rejection of me so that he may pass through a rebellious period of growth from childhood to maturity.

I should be aware, also, that I can like without loving. In a life of mere liking I restrict interest to those who potentially respond to my particular constellation of needs, fears and desires. I also refuse to grow beyond this stage of liking into true loving. In the case of exclusive liking, I meet the other only for my own satisfaction. He meets my need for adulation, protection, and self-assurance. I do nothing to foster his uniqueness, but rather perceive him only insofar as he can be a source of affection to me and increase my feelings of worth and security.

I should also realize that love is sometimes confused with only one of its possible manifestations, such as romantic feeling, sexual attraction, the intimacy of an exceptional friendship, or the affinity of two persons drawn to each other. All these manifestations are in and by themselves not the essence of human love; from them I can never learn the demands of the love we should foster for one another in community encounter.

The abuse of the word "love" has reached such proportions today that one hesitates to use it because it is so rarely understood. This confusion may lead to strange deviations in community encounter, or instill guilt in those who naturally feel dislike for certain people and mistakenly believe that they cannot encounter these fellow religious in love. I may prevent misunderstanding by temporarily substituting the word *respect* for love, meaning by respect what originally was meant by "love of neighbor." I may say that I do not wish to be loved by my fellow religious in a cheap sense, but that I wish to be respected by them. Likewise, I do not wish, nor do I feel able, to love my fellow religious in a sentimental sense, but I do wish and feel able with God's grace to respect them, independent of my impulsive sympathy and antipathy.

It is clear that God could never command the impossible — a command to spontaneously like all men and never feel any dislike for them. But He can command a respectful love which simply means that I *will* the growth and development of the other in spite of what may be an abiding dislike for his style of life, thought, and sentiment. This realization is especially important when I am called to be a superior in my community. My main task then is to create, maintain, and develop favorable conditions for the growth and unfolding of each individual religious. If I am to succeed, I must first be aware that I can profoundly dislike a considerable number of fellow religious who are quite different from me in culture, temperament, thought-patterns, and life-style. Only when I admit to myself my impulsive aversion can I guard against the intrusion of this invincible antipathy into my respect for them on the personal level. I love them when, in spite of my emotional repugnance, I respect them and continually create the right conditions for the growth of their own style of life, their own way of thought, and their own calling — all of which may be thoroughly alien to mine. On the other hand, in my dealing with the few toward whom I feel a spontaneous sympathy and affinity, my respect for them will guard against a distortion of love and justice under the influence of this prepersonal emotional element.

When I am clearly aware of my prepersonal feelings of sympathy and antipathy, I will foster the growth of my fellow religious on the personal level of encounter by not letting these lower needs in both of us dominate our relationship exclusively. Thus dialogue with my prepersonal feelings does not lead to a repression or denial of them but to a transcendence of them.

Mature human life implies the ability to live peacefully in the polarities of the normal tensions which balance personality. As long as I am immature, in moments of weakness or tiredness, I shall be tempted to escape this wholesome tension by attempting to live community encounter either on an angelic, isolated level of the spirit — the purely personal, or on the level of the prepersonal — of simple likes or dislikes. Thus, I shall tend to simplify community encounter by denying one of its essential aspects: either the personal or the prepersonal. Mine may be the mistaken belief that the repression of the awareness of one of the poles of encounter may lead to peace. True peace can come only when I am able to accept reality as it is with its tensions and polarities and surrender to the mysterious presence of the Holy who allows this polarity to be. The false peace which I achieve by cutting off the awareness of an aspect of life is a deceptive calm liable to be shattered when, in spite of my repression, I become aware of the actualities in my existence. Moreover, the very act of repression implies an anxious, unconscious investment of energy to build up elaborate defenses protecting me against any experience that threatens to bring to the fore one or the other repressed pole of encounter.

Prepersonal likes and dislikes are all part of what I may call the infrastructural aspect of encounter. The word *infrastructure* implies that the prepersonal level has a structure of its own which should not be the final structure of encounter. Over and above this is a superstructure, or personal dimension, developed in dialogue with my fellow religious, my cultural participants in the world, and the people entrusted to my care. In the religious community I live with people representing a wide variety of personal infrastructures. While I may experience a certain likeness with some, I will probably not find others in the community who have precisely the same impulsive inclinations as I do. For example, the temperament of a musician usually differs from that of a bursar. No amount of Christian love can alter such infrastructures or prevent the musician from being bored when compelled to converse with the bursar about banking procedures.

Outside the community, where my calling as participative religious is primarily situated, I am especially available for those fellowmen who share my infrastructural affinity and for whom I witness that one can live this specific spontaneity in a field of culture for the Holy. Therefore, it is by no means exceptional that a religious may at times experience a more satisfying encounter in his field of cultural participation than in his community. Community encounter has a different function in his life than his cultural encounter in the world. Community encounter should restore the religious celibate to his openness for the transcendent dimension of his cultural task by granting him the inspiration of fellow religious who may be different from him in most other aspects of life. This very difference may safeguard the primary purpose of community encounter. If all the members of a participative religious community had a similar family background and culture, a likeness in life-style and temperament, they might be tempted to make emotional and social togetherness a primary interest at the expense of their true primary dedication to the culture to which they are sent by the Lord. The acceptance of infrastructural differences will make this inversion less likely and will provide a natural stimulus to be concerned chiefly with fellow religious as unique cultural participants in the field to which each one is called.

It may be interesting to note as an aside that each religious celibate, like every human being, also has his own prepersonal disposition profile for sin. My peculiar inclination for special sins may depend again on physiological factors, early life experiences, and temperament. For example, I may come from a family where the emotional inclination to steal is so foreign that I never feel inclined to take things that are not mine. If I were locked in a jewelry store by myself, I would not be tempted to pick up one precious gem. I can take no credit for having developed this virtue; I simply lack the infrastructural predispositions necessary for the experience of the temptation to steal. The religious life attracts people with a variety of sinful predispositions. Each religious celibate is likely to be tempted and to sin in his own way. This insight may help me to be less condemning of fellow religious and more cautious of hidden pride about my own virtues. I do not know how strong the predispositions for a certain sin may be in a fellow religious, nor do I know how much my so-called virtue is simply the result of the absence of a predisposition for a certain kind of vice.

Formal Aspect of Community Encounter

Thus far we have considered four dimensions of community encounter, in-being and counter-being, personal (superstructural) and prepersonal (infrastructural), and the polarities in which they are lived. The only aspect yet to be considered is the formal expression of encounter, the peripheral shell, which is as essential a part of true encounter as its four inner dimensions. To be sure, the formal aspect would be meaningless and void without the rich interplay of these inner constituents. I first learn about the formal embodiment of encounter in my culture or my religious community. Only later am I able to appropriate it as mine by increasingly vitalizing the formal through my own experience and presence. If I isolate the formal structure of encounter from its interiority, I put myself in a lifeless position which is worse than a regression to the prepersonal level of encounter. Mere formal interaction is not prepersonal but impersonal, and cannot of itself prepare for real encounter as prepersonal experience can.

The incarnation of encounter demands a formal structure of customs, language symbols, and bodily expressions that can be understood by all in the culture or community concerned. For example, a cordial welcome may be expressed by shaking hands in America, by embracing in France, or by rubbing noses among Eskimos. I do not choose these expressions; I find them waiting for me in the culture. I can appropriate them, animate them with my own life, and express them in my own unique way, but nevertheless I am bound by them. If I use the expression of a different culture and attempt, for example, to rub noses with a guest visiting my community, I shall be misunderstood no matter how much I desire this symbol to express my personal feeling for him. I am so bound to formal structures of encounter that even in the highly spiritualized encounter of common worship, I cannot escape the necessity of formal liturgical structures which have the same meaning for all the faithful participating in this celebration. Whether I like it or not, I have to embody my encounter in some kind of formal structure.

The word "formal" may be misleading. As an American I am proud of my informality. But, actually, the formality of American encounter is *informality*. What is called informality is not the absence of structures of encounter; American forms of encounter merely differ from structures of encounter practiced in certain European societies. As an American I adhere to a code of encounter which obliges me to convey the feeling that I am not any better than the fellow next door, that I always have a sunny disposition when I meet you, that you and I are "regular fellows" who smile happily upon each other in the mutual expression of how common we are. If I were to sin against this code and break the formality of American encounter, I would be frowned upon as much as European aristocrats would frown upon those who violate their formal code of encounter. Therefore, a foreigner who wishes to be accepted soon learns the easy smile, the jovial handshake, the familiar use of the first name, and the good natured expression of the pretense that we are "all together in the same boat." The faster he learns these rules of encounter, the more acceptable he will be in his new surroundings. Formal structures of encounter are unavoidable even if I imagine myself to be free from them.

Not only does this formal structure differ from culture to culture but also from subculture to subculture. For example, the formal structure of encounter prevailing among enlisted men in the army differs from that among people who spend their lives in dedication to the fine arts. If the latter were to live among enlisted men and stubbornly maintain the encounter structures of their former milieu, they would scarcely be able to encounter at all. This formal aspect of encounter is so basic that I cannot succeed in my encounter with a culture or subculture if I do not absorb its main encounter structures.

Now, it is the essence of my vocation to worship the Lord and to witness for Him by true encounter with the specific subculture to which I am called. Therefore, I must assimilate the main structures of this subculture. Consequently, one of the greatest threats to my efficiency within the culture would be the development of a rigid community subculture which would make it difficult for me to enter into the structures of the subculture in which I must insert myself.

While a religious community needs a certain common denominator of formal encounter to facilitate mutual interaction within the community, it should never expect to eliminate all traces of the encounter structure which each one of us daily lives in the various cultural areas in which we participate. The truly participative religious community develops an unusual tolerance for the variety of encounter structures which dominate our daily lives. Here again, the possibility of retirement into one's private quarters within the community and a high respect for each other's life style are necessary to make community life tolerable among highly specialized, self-reliant men or women occupied in a variety of subcultures. Otherwise, community would become a place of exhaustive attempts to play roles in order to adjust to one another instead of being a source of relaxed renewal and joyful recollection.

Moreover, a fascinating variety of manners, language, and encounter structures has educational value insofar as it offers a possibility for each community member to acquaint himself with the style of encounter that prevails in cultural areas where he himself is not called to live his cultural-religious life. Community experience can grant him an openness and flexibility which may be indirectly useful to him in the subculture which he is serving. For example, a religious participating in the culture of an underdeveloped minority group may learn from other religious in his community how to meet with people of the different cultural strata in which they participate. This knowledge may help him to contact administrators, donors, or advisors who may be of assistance to him in his own work.

Relationship between the Formal and Other Aspects of Encounter

In relation to the infrastructure of encounter, formal encounter presents me with a necessary protection. I have seen that strong impulses and passions play a role in the infrastructural ground of encounter. The active presence of these forces may endanger the personal aspect of encounter and its moderating light. If this happens, I may say or do things which are uncharitable or unwise, and which deeply hurt my fellow religious, cultural participants, or the people entrusted to my care. Later regret may not heal the rift initially created. One of the functions of formal encounter structures is to protect me against this dangerous break in relationships because of an explosion of prepersonal feelings. Under this aspect, encounter structures are known as politeness, tact, or gentlemanly behavior. The more I assimilate the code of polite manners, the better I am protected against the dangers of my impulses breaking through. This does not mean, however, that I should repress my awareness of such impulses.

Gentleness, politeness, and gracious manners are probably more necessary in the religious community than in any other type of community. A participative religious community is an attempt by people with a variety of temperaments, backgrounds, and subcultures to live together for a lifetime without losing their individual uniqueness, which alone enables them to be profoundly useful for the work of the Lord in the culture. This unusual project of togetherness will necessarily lead to tensions. These in turn are apt to activate prepersonal passions, anxieties, and impulses which by their very nature tend to overwhelm the personal aspect of mutual encounter and may easily lead to thoughtless outbursts. The community project of coexistence can succeed only if each member masters a high degree of politeness and gentlemanly behavior, realizing that by breaking such a code he may destroy a necessary condition of community life.

The relationship between the formal and the personal aspect in meeting my fellow religious or cultural participants also requires further consideration. I have seen that in true encounter the unique and personal level should illuminate, permeate, and elevate my prepersonal passions and impulses without destroying them. When I mature as a religious, I discover in greater depth my unique calling. However, what I am is very vulnerable in its uniqueness; it is easily misunderstood or abused, and may even give rise to destructive perceptions among the people around me. If I publicly reveal my deepest self, I risk harming its quiet unfolding in the light of the Holy. The inner mystery of my being unfolds itself only in the sanctuary of my hidden life. Here, silence and recollection should reign. When I talk profusely about the motivations of my existence, they lose their fineness, and easily spoil under the curious eyes and hasty judgments of others. Moreover, I shall never be able to express fully the subtle, refined, and mysterious experiences which emerge in the depth of my personality when I live in intimacy with the Holy. Therefore, every expression of my inner life is already a failed expression. When I reveal my interiority in the glaring light of community publicity, my very communication will be influenced by my awareness that I am putting myself on display. This awareness tends to distort my communication and may help to foster a trend toward religious exhibitionism. When such a trend takes over in a community, religious may eagerly compete in soul-baring and emotional self-revelation. Such indiscriminate self-exposure is harmful whether I communicate my highest motivations or reveal the seamy side of my life. I am not only a mystery of goodness, but also a mystery of iniquity. I should keep the last as much to myself as the first, and for the same reasons. Nobody else, surely not a whole community, can ever understand the extent and meaning of sin, weakness, and failure in my life.

People who constantly communicate the innermost aspects of their being become weak and hollow men;

their inner life can never settle; it evaporates in the thin air of endless talk and sentimental commiseration. Therefore, it is unwise to apply to novitiate, seminary, or community life certain *unmitigated* types of group therapy. Such techniques may have value for people with specific problems who come together for a certain period of time under professional guidance. When the same technique is applied routinely in a religious community, the effects may be pernicious because, as we have seen, the essential spirit of the authentic religious community is a spirit of abiding respect for each individual religious as a unique mystery in which the Holy manifests itself. Imprudent soul-baring may destroy this mutual respect among people who have to live together for a lifetime and who have to develop the virtue of not interfering in the personal development of a fellow religious. To be sure, this virtue is a central life project in which the religious grows every day by inner mortification of his thought, judgment, and feeling about the other's situation and motivation. The exhibitionism described above could be a source of severe temptation to judge one another. What is worse, it could remain a lasting temptation when serious life experiences have been revealed, for example, during the novitiate or postulancy. Removed from their proper context, these revelations may make an overwhelming impression on other novices or seminarians, who may never forget and may secretly hold them against the sister, priest, or brother in later life.

We may consider the case of a person who happened to be in a seminary, novitiate, or postulancy during a period of excitement about group therapy. Seduced by the contagious mood of exalted self-revelation, he may have profoundly outshone others in this outward manifestation of humility. He may have related in group therapy sessions, for example, a sexual experience which he had before entering the novitiate. Later, however, the person concerned may have felt extremely uncomfortable about the success he scored in the unconscious competition about who could best and most humbly reveal himself. He may suspect that his fellow religious have forgotten about his praiseworthy humility but not about the saucy details of his story. He may feel as if they will always hold it against him, at least interiorly, and he may be right. Therefore, instead of fostering group therapy in the strict sense in the novitiate, or allowing professional psychotherapists to conduct public confession sessions, those in charge should protect their young and inexperienced candidates from revealing anything publicly that they may later regret. The phase of initiation into religious life is a period during which the future religious should learn to keep to himself the sacred secrets of his own inner being and should learn to avoid prying into this sacred dimension of another's being.

Thus, the personal aspect of encounter does not mean that I should publicly reveal what is most personal in my life, nor does it mean that my meeting with the other is merely prepersonal or impulsive or merely impersonal or formal. Rather it means that my personal respect for the self of the other plays its role in accordance with the situation. In other words, the style, degree, and expression of this element of personal respect should vary with the encounter situation. My encounter with the sister cook in order to secure poached eggs for breakfast should differ from my encounter with a fellow religious to express sympathy over the sudden death of a member of her family. In both encounters my personal presence should come through, but in different ways. When receiving the culinary masterpiece of the cook, I am not cold and impersonal, but in cordially thanking her, I express the respectful realization that she is a human being, a fellow religious, and not an impersonal cooking machine producing poached eggs on an assembly line. On the other hand, I would be quite out of touch with the real situation if I were to overwhelm the cook every morning with tearful demonstrations of my love for her as a fellow religious. In the situation of expressing my sympathy to the bereaved religious, on the other hand, it is not out of place to offer a warm expression of concern.

When religious become temporarily excited about the personal element of encounter, they are inclined to isolate and abstract this element from the concrete life situation. They sometimes lose their sense of proportion and desire to express how loving they are in a way which is out of touch with reality. The attempt may give rise to an artificial style of loving in the community which has a paradoxical effect opposite to that which was intended. Such artificiality is liable to destroy the true personal element of encounter because nobody can keep up this intense expression of love and charity at every moment of the day and in every situation. The exuberant expression of personal love thus becomes a new type of formality. It then becomes very difficult to communicate real personal concern and sympathy when I really should. The other may be inclined to perceive it simply as a part of the daily love show we perform for one another. Outside the community, in my cultural field of activity, the effect may be even more harmful, for I am likely to sicken people with my willful disposition of radiant happiness and undiluted love.

Appropriating Formal Structures of Encounter

To protect the most personal aspect of my being, and to guide my expression of respect and sympathy,

I rely on the formal structures of encounter. These structures have been developed by generations of people who have painfully experienced the self-destructive results of unbridled and indiscriminate exhibition of the personal and prepersonal in meeting with others. Alone, I could never invent the structures which effectively protect me against myself and against others in personal encounter. Traditional encounter structures refine every social meeting. They teach me how to move, dress, and speak in varied social situations. Moreover, generations of religious celibates have also developed structures that have been found to be protective of their personal life within and without the community. In many cases these customs have added a specific dimension to the usual structures of social life. For example, the style in which a religious celibate behaves at a wedding party is partly identical with the encounter structures of all wedding guests and partly different. For example, while the religious participates wholeheartedly in the eating of the wedding cake, he does not invite the girls to dance as other wedding guests may do. Life would be impossible if I had to determine for myself what the wisest, most agreeable, and most protective structures of personal encounter should be in all situations. I should be grateful and eager to learn the accumulated wisdom of generations in regard to relaxed and effective encounter.

I should develop, moreover, the art of vitalizing these structures with my personal life inspiration. When I know how to humanize the formal structures of encounter, I grow toward graciousness. Graciousness is the blending of my personal refinement and inspiration with the wisdom expressed by generations in the formal structures of encounter. True graciousness appears when the personal and the structural in human encounter are so deeply interwoven that the personal becomes structural and the structural personal. The formal beauty of encounter is worn as an exquisite dress that expresses beautifully every personal movement. The formal is no longer an armor that shields me from the other; it has become transparent. It lets my personal inspiration come through in a way which is not threatening, overwhelming, or unduly revealing, but agreeable and acceptable in my cultural and religious surroundings.

We have stressed repeatedly that the participative religious community is a meeting place for a surprising variety of personalities, talents, and temperaments. Moreover, it fosters each person in his very uniqueness so that he can be an effective cultural participant in the world. Life in community can be valuable only if we are protected against the power of one another's uniqueness by formal structures of encounter which we live graciously and which prevent us from over-imposing on one another. Formal structures in and by themselves can be deadening; therefore, religious should strive to grow in graciousness. What is more beautiful than a community of unique individuals living serenely in profound respect for one another's individuality, a respect which is expressed and symbolized in the gracious style in which they allow one another to be?

11

Community And The Forms Of Encounter

Diplomacy and Honesty

One of the principles influencing the development of respectful, gracious encounter is that of *diplomacy.* This may sound distasteful to me because of the widespread abuse of diplomacy: the deceptive manifestation of refined manners merely to reach a selfish goal, or a game of subtle seduction. Undoubtedly, diplomatic manners have been used to deceive others and to gain their collaboration for actions they do not desire to do. But paradoxically, the abuse of diplomacy is a demonstration of its worth. A diplomatic manifestation of selfless interest, which carefully takes into account all aspects of a life situation and of the personality of others, is so attractive and effective that even the unscrupulous egotist and crass opportunist must pay homage to it if only by imitating its outward appearances to further self-centered ends. Like every virtue, diplomacy can be used to veil evil intentions and selfish purposes.

Authentic diplomacy is the art of wisely evaluating relevant aspects of reality in myself, in others, and in our situation, insofar as these aspects are related to the best *possibility* of human encounter and of laboring together toward some desirable goal. In this sense, diplomacy is the art of the possible in obedience to reality as allowed by the Lord. Diplomacy, moreover, entails behavior that, without being dishonest or treacherous, is attuned to the sensitivities of fellow religious or cultural participants in order to avoid hurting them unnecessarily, or evoking their anxieties, impulses, and passions on the prepersonal level. I may refuse to be tactful and diplomatic under the pretext of honesty. Formal encounter and gentle behavior may be foreign to me because I have a warped notion of forthrightness. I may feel that a polite, respectful manner does not allow me to express what I really think. I should ask myself whether my passion for frankness comes from the Spirit speaking in the personal core of my being or from the dark region of my prepersonal self-centered anxieties, needs, and impulses. Is my so-called frankness and above-board behavior a screen for my refusal to be open in obedience to the many subtle aspects of my life situation and in charity to the manifold sensitivities of others around me? Do I refuse to accept God's will as revealed to me in my concrete life situation and in the other as God allows him to be? Do I disobey God's voice as speaking in reality, and interpret the situation according to my own simple specifications without caring whether or not I am responding to what is really present?

Sometimes I am tempted to simplify life to such a degree of clarity that I escape the demanding insight that all virtues are a matter of lifelong growth and development. It would be pleasant to say that I have fully acquired a virtue and then sit back and enjoy my virtue and maturity. But I would be deceiving myself. This is especially true of the virtue of honesty. To speak truthfully in encounter is one of the fundamental projects of life in which I can never succeed completely. I may approximate speaking truthfully by drawing upon my experiences as they emerge in daily encounter with others in my life situation, but truthful communication is at best a rare and difficult accomplishment. It implies that I succeed in making the other really experience what I myself experience and desire to share with him. It is not merely a matter of using customary words, but of discovering whether or not these words have the same meaning for him as they do for me. I have to grow daily in refined attention to the other's world of meaning in order to find words which will not lead to misunderstanding and untruth, but to real comprehension of what I desire to express. Tragically, what superficially seems to be true communication may be untrue in its effects. For example, I may wish to communicate to a fellow religious that moderate progress in the development of religious life is good. Do I stop to consider that in his world the word progress may conjure up images of wild-eyed reformers intruding on the sanctuary of religious life and blindly destroying sacred traditions? On the other hand, I may attempt to communicate to another religious my conviction that true progress is only possible in the light of a respect for tradition, without realizing that he experiences a rise in blood pressure when he hears the word *tradition*. Because of his particular emotional background, tradition means staleness, repression, and absence of any progress. Therefore, instead of effecting truth in my communication, I serve untruth. My fellow religious now has an untrue image of what faithfulness to tradition really means to me.

I may have a similar experience in encounter with my coworkers and with those entrusted to my care. Perhaps I wish to communicate to them the beauty of true religious experience by using words of traditional piety. It may be that their emotional mood and background are such that they do not understand in the least the beauty of mature religious experience. My words remind them of a saccharine kind of piety on the prepersonal level of existence whose purpose, like an insurance policy, is to quiet fears about the future. My lack of ability to communicate the truth, in spite of my best intentions, only serves to reinforce in them a revolt against a religion which they believe to be out of touch with reality.

The virtue of truthfulness and honesty is not an adherence to an abstract concept. It must be incarnated in daily attempts to grow toward more effective human ways of communicating what I really want to say. The religious who is called to communicate truth in encounter with people whose culture may be alienated from religion should develop the sensitivity necessary to communicate truth effectively. Such a population is composed of a variety of personalities and is in need of an art of communication which is sensitive to the times but not sensational — an art of communication which strives diligently to speak the truth and does not thrive on arousing the fearful, misinformed, and prejudiced beliefs of whatever audience may be listening.

Principle of Respectful Distance

Among the principles of external structuring of encounter which we have learned from the study of formal modes of being together, we have discussed diplomacy and honesty. Another principle which is even more basic in the structuring of forms of encounter is that of respectful distance. The necessity for respectful distance is deeply rooted in the fundamental structure of man. As a matter of fact, it is so essential to his nature that it is already foreshadowed in animal life. When it is neglected, physical, psychological, and social disturbances result. Scientists have related psychosomatic symptoms in people working in factories to the lack of minimum respectful distance. For example, when a supervisor was literally breathing down the necks of employees, strange headaches and stomach disturbances resulted. The most effective remedy was the maintenance of a proper distance.

Similarly, in religious communities when respectful distance is not maintained and privacy is not guaranteed, many symptoms may appear. A dissatisfaction with religious life is experienced; inner peace and prayerfulness are lost; tension, irritation, moodiness, and tiredness appear without apparent cause. Some religious may even leave the community, feeling that somehow life there is unbearable. They may ascribe this feeling to painful memories of an unhappy childhood, their own sinfulness, difficulties with superiors, loss of union with God, temptations against celibacy, or lack of interest in their daily task. It may be, however, that in certain cases these symptoms are secondary to the main cause: an abiding lack of privacy and distance, the basic need of which is so profoundly bound up with the very structure of human nature. In sensitive people, this lack of privacy may lead to an unconscious bio-psychological revolt accompanied by certain of the symptoms described.

The principle of respectful distance and privacy must be maintained in religious life. Indeed, this principle must find greater application in a religious community than in any other. People in other social groups are not obliged to live with the same individuals for a lifetime in the intimacy of a shared home without being family members. Religious courageously dare to bind themselves together for life, promising to develop their unique personalities and indeed promoting in one another the highest possible development of their uniqueness. Such an ideal is difficult to achieve when the principle of respectful distance is not guaranteed by formal encounter structures.

The respectful distance which protects privacy is so fundamental that we can study traces of it in animal life. Robert Ardrey has written a book about animals called *The Territorial Imperative*. The territorial principle in animal life foreshadows that of respectful privacy in the life of a human community. If one animal invades the territory of another, the one intruded upon becomes aggressive or defensive. Fight or flight follows. In community life, unnecessary intrusion on the privacy of a religious is liable to arouse similar bio-psychological aggressive or defensive attitudes. The organism of the person may tighten up, unconsciously readying him for fight or flight. On the conscious level, however, his desire to be humble and charitable inclines him to smilingly repress the awareness of his keyed-up body. Therefore, recognition of his tension does not lead to release. His bio-psychological organization may become so taut that he experiences tiredness, exhaustion, dissatisfaction, and depression. Even worse, the evoked aggressiveness may turn inward and lead to abnormal guilt feelings, scrupulosity, or tortured forms of asceticism.

If the religious is overly sensitive to disrespectful intrusions on his privacy because of the lack of formal encounter structures, he may live almost constantly under the pressure of bio-psychological forces. Persisting psychosomatic symptoms such as high blood pressure, nervous headaches, and recurring ulcers are not uncommon. There may even be a correspondence between the lack of respectful distance in the community and the incidence of virus infections which help to populate the infirmary.

If such bio-psychological energies cannot be released, they not only exhaust the body but diminish the energy which could be invested in full cultural participation in the world. Of course, intrusion into privacy cannot be totally avoided. Incidental intrusions do not harm me provided they are clearly recognized and condemned as such in the light of the formal encounter structures of my community. Supported by a common refusal to bear with such lack of respect, I am able to relieve the tension which is its necessary consequence. But constant desecration of privacy because of the absence of appropriate encounter structures is a serious handicap to community spirit, and even more so to the personality development of the insensitive intruder himself.

Of course, it is possible to condition people in novitiates and seminaries to live without privacy. Moreover, a sentimental prepersonal "encounter" movement, indulging the childish desire for total in-being, can promote the fantasy that we should eliminate distance or privacy. Human gullibility may espouse such wishful thinking. But not for long. The privacy-imperative stirs up forces within me when others constantly trespass on my personal life. Whether I approve or disapprove, whether I like it or not, it is a demand of my nature that I cannot escape.

The need for privacy and distance is a force rooted so deeply in my personality and my organism that I have no knowledge of its origin. When I study the primates, I see that many of them have found a way of living together under the pressure of this instinct. They have developed formal structures of contact which foreshadow the free structures of encounter developed by man. Many primates maintain distance from one another apparently by structures of simple avoidance passed on from generation to generation. In some species of animals, it may happen that an intrusion on private territory comes about accidentally. Peace is maintained not so much by the failure of the animal whose privacy has been disturbed to fight off the disrespectful intruder, but by the instinct of the intruding animal itself to withdraw. As soon as it discovers its violation of the unwritten law of peaceful togetherness, it withdraws swiftly and effectively, seemingly embarrassed by its own mistake.

I may compare this example with a similar embarrassed reaction in human beings when they intrude upon another's privacy by accident in situations which are so clearly personal that they cannot escape a feeling of shame. This primitive, almost instinctual respect, is experienced in situations in which the material bodily privacy of the other is violated. As a human being, however, I should develop a greater sensitivity for the psychological and spiritual privacy of the other. When a fellow religious is absent, and I ask disrespectful questions about where he is and what he is doing, I should feel greater embarrassment than I felt in the case of an accidental intrusion upon his bodily privacy. In an authentic community, every member develops this sensitivity to such a degree that all feel uneasy when anyone pries into another's work, acquaintances, spiritual life, unique life style, or family relationships. Formal structures of encounter embody the behavior which naturally flows from this sensitivity. They protect against prepersonal impulses and compulsions of vulgar curiosity.

Fundamental to the principle of respect for privacy are two opposing impulses: my prepersonal urge to intrude on the personal life of my fellow religious because of anxiety and insecurity, and the urge to avoid intrusion because of respect. My need for excitement or security may sometimes swing the balance in favor of intrusion. If, on the other hand, my life as a participative religious is interesting because of my commitment to my daily tasks in the world, and if my insecurity in regard to the possible successes of my fellow religious is replaced by a sense of security which I find in myself as a unique manifestation of the Holy, then the balance will swing in favor of avoidance of intrusion. To be sure, when the organismic impulse to avoid intrusion prevails in my life, I do not yet live on the proper human level which transcends impulse and compulsion. I can grow in the virtue of respect for privacy by liberating myself from the fear that dominates all my attitudes on the prepersonal level. Gradually, I shall be able to commit myself freely to respectful appreciation of the other because of his human dignity, not simply because avoidance of intrusion happens to be the best means to prevent unpleasantness. I shall respect the supernatural dignity of my fellow religious who, as a person, is elevated by grace, redeemed by the Lord, and called by the Holy Spirit to be a unique expression of Christ in the world.

The Aggressive Impulse

Respect for the integrity of my fellow religious is endangered by my inclination to impose myself, my perceptions, and my ideals on those who are by nature weak, shy, dependent, and insecure. They do not dare to oppose disrespectful demands of fellow religious, especially when spoken in the seductive language of a soft appeal to charity or humility. The inclination to abuse weaker personalities in the community may be related to the intraspecies aggressiveness discussed by Konrad Lorenz in his book, *On Aggression.* The original meaning and purpose of aggressiveness, according to Lorenz, was to enhance the natural selection of the best animals so that the species could continue, even at the expense of killing off or relegating to an inferior position those animals that were weak, ineffective, or a hindrance to the development of the species.

We may still find traces of this primitive inclination in man when he lives in community. Over the centuries, religious communities have devised rules, regulations, and structures which curb this primitive drive in more powerful personalities who strive unconsciously to impose their ideas, customs, and projects on fellow religious who find it difficult to refuse cooperation. The wisdom embodied in community rules protects religious against their inclination to violate the integrity of one another by imposition. I may be presently enjoying this necessary protection without realizing that this benefit comes to me from community rules. There may be a split in my self-experience because I have repressed the awareness of deep-seated bio-psychological impulses which are present as dynamic forces within me. Mine may be an angelic view of the human person, a view which is self-deceiving and dangerous. I may, for instance, deny the reality of the intraspecies aggressiveness which is present in each one of us. As a consequence of this denial, I may propose that we do away with certain structures, unaware that they protect us against this impulse of aggressiveness. I may claim that we should substitute instead a life of angelic love for one another.

Some communities have allowed small groups to

carry on this experiment with interesting results. In sly ways, the age-old instinct to overpower the weak took over. Soon the energetic religious, the great talents, the big voices were in control. The personalities of, let us say, six strong, determined religious were so convincing, reasonable, and enthusiastic that they easily seduced the two more modest religious to betray their own needs, life style, and interest. The refined logic and attractive idealism, the shining holiness and good intentions of the more aggressive religious, soon tricked the modest ones into believing that they themselves really consented to the projects of the others. Thus the less outspoken religious became self-alienated and self-estranged. They no longer lived as the unique persons they could be in their own right, under the personal inspiration of the Holy Spirit, but they simply lived the life of the six religious "powerhouses" who subtly overwhelmed them with their projects and ideals. Indeed, the influence was so subtle that those concerned did not even realize that the privacy and integrity of the less assertive religious were intruded upon.

No human being and no human community can live without structures. When I take away the clearly defined structures of a common rule, they will be replaced by uncontrollable implicit structures which will be subtly suggested or loudly proclaimed by fellow religious who are aggressive, convincing, clever personalities, and who unconsciously restructure the so-called structureless community in their own image. The worst effect is that the shy or less talented religious is no longer protected against the cleverness, enthusiasm, and holy projects of the strong or sly personalities. Forming a clan of puritans or idealists, they draw the less sophisticated religious into their vision, even if it is disagreeable to the deepest personalities of those seduced.

Hence, when I study the encounter structures of my community as embodied in certain rules and customs, I should always ask how far these structures protect the privacy of each member and how far they defend us against one another, especially against those powerful personalities who are unconsciously inclined to force their projects upon others. Consider, for example, the rules of silence. Each active religious community protects the privacy and integrity of each one of its members by allowing everyone the right to be silent at certain times or places when all others are forbidden to intrude upon him. If everyone had the right to intrude on my silence and recollection at any time of the day or night, how vulnerable I would be! If I happen to be a strong personality and do not care about loss of popularity, I may frankly tell the intruder to leave me alone. If I am, moreover, psychologically astute I can recognize his subtle play on my generosity. The religious community, however, is not meant to be a place for only strong and sophisticated personalities able to defend their dignity against powerful or clever intruders. I may be the type of person who hesitates to tell others that I wish to be alone. Or, in the name of charity and availability. I may prostitute my best self in order to satisfy the insensitive demands of others upon my time, energy, and opportunities of recollection. If there are no community structures to protect me, I shall be unable to resist infringement upon my personality by the pious fast talkers, community jokers, and overly dependent religious who make excessive demands on my time and energy. The eternally new projects of other "creative" religious may imply endless hours of talking and allow no time or place for silence and recollection. It would be difficult to conceive of living a lifetime, day and night, with all types of personalities, without the protection of structures. A community lacking formal encounter structures which are objective, rather than dictated by the whims of various insensitive personalities, will sooner or later become a place of torment for the more modest and refined personality. In spite of the best intentions of the "loud" personality, intraspecies aggressiveness will assert itself in time if the modest are not protected by encounter structures incorporated in stable rules.

Disrespectful Intrusion

Even within a community which protects the privacy of each individual by rules, disrespectful intrusion may still occur. It is a danger which is never totally absent. One manifestation of intrusion is the urge to pry into the private life of a fellow religious. Here the urge to peek finds its most disturbing manifestation — not in the superficial area of bodily exposure, but in the realm of psychological, personal and spiritual intimacy.

Any community may contain these perverted peekers devoured by the need to pry into the life of their fellow religious. The impertinently inquisitive religious may be identified by many psychological symptoms. He is the first to seek information about his fellow religious who is absent from the community. If a rumor is abroad about a fellow religious, the peeker's reaction is indicative of his perversion. He can scarcely hide his eagerness to hear every detail of the story. Normally uninterested, perhaps somewhat bored with real news, he is strangely elated by this electrifying bit of gossip. Only rumors can stimulate him.

The devouring inclination to be a peeping tom can be found in people who have an urge to share secretly, without commitment and responsibility, the bodily intimacy of another. Sometimes this may be a sexual perversion due to certain circumstances which are not rooted in the structure of the personality as a whole. In others it may be a real deviation that affects not only the sexual dimension of the human personality but the personality in its total life orientation. In that case we deal with a peeping tom in the psychological sense. The psychological foundation for such an intense, irresistible need to pry continuously is the lack of intimacy with himself. Lacking both the inner resources of a rich personal life and the absorbing joy of being called by the Holy and dedicated to a unique mission, he suffers from an all-pervading boredom and loneliness which call out for relief. The way to fill his empty life with meaning would be to commit himself wholeheartedly to God, to his task, and to others. But for reasons which probably revert to early childhood experiences, he fears this active involvement. He has no trust in his ability to make his own life exciting and meaningful. He has paralyzed his potentiality for admiration and respect with the implied loss of ever being able to enjoy the achievement of the other. Lacking the inspiring intimacy with the Holy which comes with the acceptance of solitude, he is unable to rise from meaninglessness by means of a holy commitment to his life task and his fellowman. He tries unconsciously to substitute for intimacy with the Holy a passive artificial intimacy through vicarious participation in another's intimate life. The peeping attitude among religious will not usually lead to the superficial infringement upon the intimacy of the other by looking secretly at his exposed body. He preys upon a far more personal and holier intimacy than the superficial external intimacy of the body. The religious peeping tom is inclined to pry into the most secret recesses of the personal life of his fellow religious. His curiosity about what they are thinking, doing, feeling, and hoping drives him to subtle questioning, shrewd observations, and secret rumor-spreading in the hope that others will bear out his prejudices and reward him with revealing remarks.

While the superficial peeping tom limits his activities to an occasional glimpsing of the bodily intimacy of one or the other person, the religious peeping tom is daily preoccupied with rumors and exciting stories about the faults and the doubtful morality of fellow celibates. Their life becomes his life and his daily excitement. While the superficial bodily peeping tom can satisfy his abnormal craving only on certain unusual occasions, the religious peeping tom can be engaged in this mode of existence for hours.

When his psychological illness is grave, professional therapy is required. Less serious cases may be able to seek help from a good spiritual director, provided the structures of encounter in the community can protect him against his own unsavory inclination. A religious community is safe from the religious peeping tom when its atmosphere is such that every member frowns immediately upon the person who makes a remark or asks a question which reveals a lack of respect or the presence of an insolent curiosity. An authentic community, in which each member is deeply convinced that impertinent transgression of the boundaries of personal privacy is a serious peril for the community spirit, offers the best hope of recovery from this unwholesome inclination provided that it has not yet taken possession of the personality as a whole.

Identity, Stimulation, and Security

It is clear that religious should never invade the privacy of one another by breaking the formal code of respectful encounter — a code built up by humanity through the experience of generations. I can only understand the strange urge to violate privacy in the light of certain basic needs of man which somehow have not been fulfilled in a positive, constructive, and deeply satisfying way. According to Robert Ardrey, the fundamental needs of men are for identity, stimulation, and security. The religious is not alien to these human needs. If I am honest I must admit that deep within myself I shun anonymity; I want to be somebody in the eyes of God, myself, and others. I also dread boredom; I yearn for stimulation, meaning, and excitement. Finally, I seek to dispel the anxiety that emerges in me at various times in my life; I seek security. The extent of these needs in me is dependent on the degree of identity, stimulation, and security which I experienced as a child, and which remains with me as a lasting experience of my potentialities in this regard. Some needs may be more pressing than others, but usually the need for identity is most powerful. This need was especially urgent at the time that I had not yet appropriated the common rules and customs of my community in a personal way. As long as I did not personalize these rules and customs, I felt impersonal and anonymous. I know that it is necessary that certain times or places be set aside for prayer, silence, and recollection, other times for study and meals; but it is my own responsibility to personalize my moments of recollection and prayer. I do so partly by becoming aware that the rule of prayer is good for me because it reveals to me that I am personally called by the Holy to spend my time in this way. Being at prayer does not mean that I should lose myself in the anonymity of a crowd going through liturgical motions but that in sharing the words and movements with my community, I can make my prayer both personal and communal.

Even rules and customs that I cannot experience as meaningful because of my own lack of insight, or because of a changed situation, can be appropriated as meaningful within my life project. I can, as it were, impose on them the supra-meaning of something meaningless which the Holy allows to come into my life so that I may grow as a religious by accepting all things in the spirit of surrender to the Holy Wisdom that allows them to be. Such acceptance will deepen my personal surrender to Him as well as strengthen my structure-tolerance. The latter will help me even outside the community, when I as a lonely participant in the culture enter situations filled with frustrating regulations and seemingly meaningless procedures.

When I neglect my need to personalize common structures of community life, I may endanger my experience of identity and succumb to a vague anonymity. In reaction, an overpowering need for meaningful identity will automatically emerge. Not satisfying this need in myself may result in the urge to prey upon the privacy of others in a foolish attempt to live a vicarious identity.

My need for stimulation is second in importance to my need for identity. As a human being, I can grow and develop only by interaction with my environment. If I am not stimulated and challenged, my potentialities are not actualized. Soon I become bored and tired. Life loses interest. This flaccid state may lead to anxiety, depression, and despair. When stimulation is absent, I seem to realize instinctively and intuitively that my existence is in jeopardy. For animals, the only stimulation needed is biological. The stimulation of man, however, is dependent also on the world of meaning which he reveals to himself in a personal way. Therefore, as a religious, I should use my time of retreat, recollection, meditation, spiritual reading, and discussion to deepen my experience of the stimulating values in the life that I am living and the tasks that I am performing as a cultural-religious participant. When I do not engage myself in this continually renewed attempt to personalize the meaning of my tasks and my religious life, I lose touch with their stimulating power. The demon of boredom may invade my existence so that I search anxiously for artificial stimulation. In religious life I may find this by unwholesome vicarious involvement in the personal lives of my fellow religious. Other artificial stimulants — drugs, alcohol, vandalism, riots, and sexual experiments — which are readily available to people outside the community who lose contact with the values in their own lives, are not readily available to me as a religious. Thus, the religious who has failed to renew himself in the experience of personalized values is in danger of seeking a cheap type of artificial stimulation in the prying attitude. For him it represents the nearest possibility of finding the real excitement he craves.

Security is man's other need. Contrary to what I may think, it is usually sacrificed for either the need for identity or stimulation when it becomes strong and demanding. There exists a curious conflict between the need for security and the need for identity and stimulation. The readiness to sacrifice security for stimulation and identity may explain the surprising behavior of religious who have lived secure lives and suddenly do something very foolish which jeopardizes their security. For example, a religious lecturer who is more or less reasonable and prudent may be seduced by an applauding crowd to make an unwise statement about religious doctrine which puts him in the headlines of the press. I do not refer, of course, to the case in which a religious after long deliberation, study, and scholarship comes to a conviction which he expresses humbly and prudently, only to find to his chagrin that he is quoted out of context by news media hungry for sensation. I refer, rather, to the person who becomes intoxicated by the heady wine of making the headlines from coast to coast. The urge to be noticed as a brilliant, or even a dangerous man, can be linked with a driving need to escape anonymity and find stimulation, even at the expense of security.

My need for security is at the root of my conservatism, my anxious care to maintain the status quo, my overdependency on my fellow religious, my craving for in-being, fear of the counter-experience, and my dread of going into the culture as a lone, self-reliant witness for the Holy. My need for security may lead to an overstructuring of my life within the community and within the culture. The more insecure I am basically, the more anxious I become about every possible element in my community which may infringe upon the structure of security that I have so carefully built. The element I may feel most uncertain about is the unique personality of each of my fellow religious. In my anxious structuring of life in the religious community, I have carefully assigned a place to each member in such a way that I am sure of his orientation, reactions, and projects. As soon as he speaks or acts differently than he should according to my security scheme, I experience anxiety. I am no longer sure that I can manipulate him in a way which will maintain my position of safety. To make things worse, his words or deeds may invoke reactions in me which threaten my own system of judgments, plans, projects, and perceptions. Constant anxiety, evoked by my lack of inner security and self-reliance, may be another cause of my steady prying into the lives of my fellow religious and of my constant transgression of their sacred privacy. Anxious that I may lose my security if I am not aware of every change taking place in the lives of the members of my community, I begin to compulsively check every detail of their behavior which may give me a clue to possible changes going on in their lives and their cultural enterprises.

The contagious force of this anxious urge may be so strong in some members of the community that only a strict adherence to formal encounter structures will protect the community spirit. On the other hand, all of us feel the same anxiety to the degree that we do not find inner security. Once more I realize my profound obligation to strengthen my inner certainty by deepening my presence to the Holy, by finding in God my true security, and by becoming aware that if I am faithful to my cultural-religious calling, He will always be infinitely more faithful to me.

Interestingly enough, when I am able to relax my anxious preoccupation with the successes, failures, problems, and changes of fellow religious, I shall have greater energy for a full presence to my own cultural-religious task. My wholehearted, undivided presence to my life project will increase my effectiveness and my production which, in turn, will lead to an increase in peripheral security. While peripheral security gained by success in my life task is not so fundamental as basic security gained in my trustful presence to the Holy, it still enhances my security accidentally and contributes correspondingly to the diminishment of my urge to pry into the life of fellow religious or to violate their sacred privacy in order to satisfy my own needs for security.

As already noted, a tension exists between my need for security and my need for identity and stimulation. My need for security may lead to an overstructuring of my personal religious life, my cultural task, and my immediate environment. This rigid organization of my existence makes me feel safe but at the same time gives rise to boredom. The more I tighten the personal structures of my religious, cultural and social life, the less I shall be able to experience my uniqueness which makes me aware of my identity. If I wish to be safe from all disapproval, rejection, misunderstanding, conflict, or decrease in popularity, I must repress all awareness of my original selfhood and abstain from every expression of individuality. The more anonymous I become, the more absorbed in a numb collectivity, the less I shall risk my acceptance and popularity. This betrayal of the Lord as unique revelation in my consecrated self will be rewarded with an overwhelming security and deadening safety insofar as they can be obtained by blind conformity to a collectivity. The cowardly religious, who is in this way unfaithful to God's personal call, finds his punishment in this life. At the moment I reach a numbing security by the highest possible anonymity, I may experience an all-pervading boredom and disgust with life, an aching need for selfhood and excitement. In some cases, as we have already seen, these needs may overpower me and lead to strange outbursts to assert myself suddenly as an individual. I may even feel tempted to leave religious life, forgetting that I myself, not the community, am primarily guilty of my deadness. More often, however, I shall become the victim of a frantic search for a vicarious thrill and a vicarious identity by intrusion on the privacy of fellow religious.

Another symptom of my deviation may be the growth of an unconscious envy of those fellow religious who have escaped the boredom of life and stand out as unique individuals, alive and energetic, renewed daily by the values in which they believe and by the cultural enterprises in which they engage. The unfortunate religious who has lost his life because he was too eager to find and secure it, experiences an aching pain when he sees fellow religious who were not afraid to follow the Lord in His suffering, rejection, and misunderstanding and who, therefore, are already rewarded in this life with the joy of truly living their personalized values. Their feeling of security is not external but deep within themselves where their identity is experienced as a continual unique gift of the Holy. Their holiness, which enabled them through grace not to shun the disapproving voices of the crowd, is a living reproach to the fellow religious who has chosen an easy, secure life and forgotten that the disciple is not better than his master. Because the self-reliant, personal religious is a reproach to the one who is anxiously submerging himself in the contagious moods, whims, and anonymity of the crowd, he necessarily evokes in the anxious one unconscious aggressive and destructive forces which the latter cannot admit to himself. The bitterness and vindictiveness which arise when he meets a fellow religious who is alive, creative, and effective has its roots partly in his need to make everyone conform to his safe and predictable life structures. A unique individual, one who is vital, happy, and open to the inspiration of the Holy, is never predictable in all aspects of his thoughts, feelings, and perceptions. He manifests the annoying unpredictability of the Lord and the saints.

This destructive force of the overly secure religious also finds root in unconscious jealousy and envy insofar as the dissatisfied religious cannot repress his awareness that the religious who is faithful to his call finds rich reward in his daily growth in inner strength. The pseudo-secure religious also experiences a deep desire to be true to himself, not to sell himself, his inner values, and his convictions in order to maintain the approval of the crowd. Another ground for his aggressiveness can be found in the final twist which may take place in his personality: values themselves are now perversely perceived as non-values, and their absence is exalted as authentic value. The overly defensive religious may claim and even believe that mediocrity is prudence, that anxious anonymity is humility, that the betrayal of the call of the Spirit is modesty, that the cowardly refusal to engage oneself is recollection, and that the need to be liked is charity. In this perversion of values, the virtues of the religious who answers the call of his Master are perceived as pride, lack of modesty, and inordinate ambition. The sick mind can develop a world of meaning in which the defensive religious feels righteous about his destructive persecution of fellow religious who are faithful to the call of the Holy. Such perverted self righteousness is a danger to community life because it justifies violation of all the formal encounter structures which protect respect for the uniqueness of the other and his call. Once these structures are publicly ignored without implicit or explicit disapproval of the other religious, a process of deterioration sets in. When the community spirit is too debilitated for a concerted action against infringement upon any of its members, others may feel tempted to the same violation. The true community spirit, which is one of respectful promotion of the uniqueness of each member, is slowly replaced by the mentality of crowd or collectivity, which dominates through fear of the disapproval of others.

Most tragic of all in such a downward development is the fact that the religious initially left family and other establishments in society in order to be free from the systematic pressures of approval and disapproval linked with the structures of society. He left them to be free for the inspiration of the Holy in the culture. This is the inner meaning of the participative religious life. What a tragic reversal if the person called to this life of freedom falls victim to the temptation of absolute security which makes him unfaithful to the unique call of the Holy.

It is true, of course, that being faithful to my uniqueness in the fulfillment of my life task and in community with my fellow religious does not necessarily mean that I do things in a peculiar way or that I do only what I like to do. In community life, the fundamental principle of respectful promotion of each member's uniqueness, far from being whimsical and individualistic, leads to rules, customs, and unwritten encounter structures which limit and discipline our individualistic, egoistic needs and desires. Indeed, the true fostering of the uniqueness of all in sacred respect means that I personally appropriate the common rule and task. I continually permeate their meaning with my personal feeling, perception, and insight into their values. Thus I grow to an awareness of personal responsibility and commitment to everything I am asked to do. My engagement as a person will necessarily lead to faithfulness and zeal, even though this may irritate those who are not thus committed — those who have not personally appropriated their task as an invitation to give themselves wholly to God's unfolding of creation as manifest in the specific area to which they are uniquely called.

12

Community Encounter And Personality Development

Encounter, as we have seen, is a phenomenon whose basic structure is the polarity between in-being and opposition, between the experience of oneness with others and that of the uniqueness of self. Encounter in community must manifest these two aspects, though they need not always be of like strength. At times, especially during my initiation into the religious community, my identification with more or less ideal fellow religious may be strongest and may stand in the foreground of my experience. Even then, however, my awareness of self should prevent absorption into the personality of the admired religious so that I will not risk losing personal conscience and responsibility. At other times, especially after my initiation into religious life, the experience of personal responsibility and unique selfhood becomes central. This may happen when I enter a cultural dimension of the world independently and participate in an original way in the progress of mankind. At this time, the task of adapting myself to a new cultural environment without losing my identity makes me profoundly aware of my uniqueness as emerging from the Holy who calls me to be an original manifestation of His presence in a particular dimension of the culture. Though the experience of my difference from others now prevails, the experience of being-in-with-others lingers in the background, for without it no encounter is possible.

In my initial acquaintance with my field of cultural activity, I may experience predominantly the counter-aspect of encounter. I may feel deeply the difference between the fundamental motivation which inspires me and that which inspires some of my cultural partners. Gradually, however, I shall become more at home with them. I may be aware not only of self-centered motivations but also of idealistic concern for the progress of mankind. When the Lord is with me and helps me to keep my intention pure, I hope that His very being in me may make others aware of this perhaps weakened but still shimmering light in the depth of their own personality. This awareness strengthens my experience of in-being with them. I am increasingly able to identify with their problems and to understand why it is so difficult for some of them to withstand the motivations for status, power, and possession which cloud their service to mankind in and through their cultural and social activities. I know that the same temptations assail me; I am not exempt from the demon of pride, from the desire for acceptance and popularity, from the devouring need for attention. I too am in danger of damaging the objective holy orientation of my cultural contribution. I am aware that I sometimes succumb to these powers in spite of the tremendous gift of religious life which offers me the possibility of recollection and of intensified presence to the Holy so that I may purify my cultural orientation. At my best moments, when the light of grace makes me aware of the darkness of my egoism, I realize that many of my cultural partners who do not enjoy this gift of religious life nevertheless struggle in their own way to protect the purity of their cultural orientation. Probably they would purify their motivations better than I do now if they were called to my life of liberation by the vows. This realization enables me to identify humbly with the numerous obstacles they meet in combating human pride and the need to be accepted at any price. I share this human situation with them and have faith that Christ our Redeemer desires to assist us all in facing the self-centered needs which hinder the full cultural-religious unfolding of His redeemed humanity.

My growth in understanding of the needs and desires I share with the rest of mankind is thus indicative of the fact that encounter truly affects my development as a religious personality. In order to understand the meaning of encounter in this respect, I may reflect on certain aspects of the basic structure of my being.

Encounter as Revelation of Myself to Myself

I *am* human presence. I am not closed in upon myself as a rock or a tree. I am primordially in the world and present to the meaning of the gestures, words, and deeds of people as no lifeless thing can be. Even as a little child I discovered myself not through my own eyes but through the eyes of my mother. Her love and appreciation was the ground of my self-love and self-appreciation. My encounter with my mother revealed me to myself. If she, or the person who took her place, never showed me love and appreciation, I cannot love myself. I can only reject myself as she rejected me, until I am redeemed from my self-loathing by a person who in loving encounter unveils to me who I am. Sometimes it is only the therapeutic encounter which can heal me from this wound of my childhood.

It is impossible to overemphasize the dynamic role that encounter plays in my life story of becoming. When I enter the religious community I do not know, nor will I ever fully know, the profile of abilities which I am, and which I should develop in the service of the Holy. I can only develop these potentialities insofar as the Lord reveals them to me in and through encounter, first with my fellow religious and later with the cultural participants who share my worldly task and with those entrusted to my care. In encounter I become aware of who I am as a person. Encounter reveals to me not only my potentialities for the good, but also the specific form which the demonic assumes in me. For example, in a heated encounter I may become aware of my possibility to be slanderous, hateful, or murderous to a degree which I never suspected. This knowledge is a great gift. My wholesome development as a human person and a religious implies a humble awareness of the unique constellation of demonic possibilities which constantly taints my religious witnessing. This self-knowledge may even be more important for my personal growth than the awareness of my potentialities for the good.

As we have seen, in the religious community we stimulate in one another the highest development of the profile of talents and human potentialities which each one of us uniquely is. Each religious in the community has committed himself to encourage his fellow religious to develop himself as far as possible so that, as a new and original light, he may shine forth in the culture — even if his service does not immediately benefit the community itself or his fellow religious. The authentic religious community has purified itself from self-centeredness. Its devouring motivation is to make Christ present in the world through the unfolding of His presence in each individual religious. My personal call reveals itself gradually as I discover my unique constellation of potentialities for the divine and for the demonic. While I foster the first, I have to protect myself against the latter so that grace may triumph in my life.

Identifying Encounter

My growth takes place in and through identifying encounter. I may never have realized this because the process may have been unconscious. In order to prevent misunderstanding, I should distinguish between authentic and unauthentic identification in my community relationships and in my meeting with others in my cultural field of presence. Only authentic identification can lead to discovery of my identity as rooted in the Holy. When I have a deep encounter with another, I identify with him as far as possible. In respect for and admiration of his qualities, I unconsciously try to be like him. In this movement of identification with a seminary director, a novice mistress, a superior, or a fellow religious, I may gradually discover how much I am alike and how much I am different from them. I may, for example, have a potentiality for the mode of meditation typical of my novice mistress. I never really knew that this possibility existed in me. Only when it is actualized and embodied in a living person, do I become aware that I too could be like this. The discovery of this potentiality of spiritual life is not a rational insight only. Mere abstract concepts cannot unfold a human life. The discovery is a true life experience, a temporary sharing in the prayer life of another. Such a sharing of a living embodiment of what is as yet only a mere possibility in me takes place in and through my whole-hearted identification with this dimension of the life of the other. Therefore, the main calling of religious educators and spiritual directors is to embody in their concrete lives what is present in the young only as an abstract ideal, a still unfuifilled expectation, a promise and a possibility. When I identify with the prayer life of my exemplar, I become gradually aware of the counter aspect of this identifying encounter. If I am truly open to the experience which the Lord grants me, then I become aware that I may identify with the prayer life of this person who is very much like me, but that my prayer can never be identical with hers. No matter how similar we are, there is always a point of difference. This is the mysterious center of my uniqueness and my special grace. Hence it is only in the attempt to identify with the other that I become acutely aware that I am not identical with her.

Unfortunately, this process of growth can be distorted by the immature religious. As we have seen, no growth is possible without some identification. But it is possible that I may enter the postulancy, novitiate, or seminary as an immature adolescent. I may still live in childish rebellion against all parent figures, or I may suffer from a neurotic anxiety that I shall lose myself if I dare to admire or identify with another. When I am tortured by neurotic rebellion or an overwhelming fear of absorption, I may try to defend myself against my need for identification. I may do so through an escape into critical discourse. From the very beginning of my initiation into religious life, I assume a haughty, rationalistic attitude. My deep-seated insecurity and anxiety incite me to sit in judgment on what is lacking in my spiritual leaders or fellow religious. I look for what they are not as compared to what I already am. It may be that my novice mistress or seminary director is experienced in the life of prayer, but my anxiety leads me to focus only on the limitations of his speech in the self-defensive awareness that I spoke much better to the student association of my high school or college than he does to us novices or seminarians. This defensive nihilism also permeates my attitude toward those around me who are called by the Lord to be initiated into the same community. Instead of discovering, admiring, and identifying with their assets — perhaps their beautiful readiness to identify with the ideals of religious life as embodied in my religious mentors — I unconsciously desire only to be irritated by what they do not possess: their lack of sophistication, their worldly inexperience, their naivete in matters in which I happen to be up to date. Dwelling only on their limitations, on what they are not, I live constantly in a sphere of "nothingness" or negativity which necessarily leads to emptiness in my own life. I begin to live in proud isolation from others. In such a mood, true encounter and identification are impossible, growth is stunted, and the discovery of my own possibilities for religious life is withheld from me. Instead of growing into a graceful religious, I grow into a disgraceful critic unable to encounter others. What is worse, I may try unconsciously to seduce my seminary director or novice mistress to leave the field of true encounter where real growth takes place and to engage with me in rationalistic dialogue about the limitations of the community and the other seminarians or novices. If I am not able to break through my wall of defensive superiority, then the greatest gift I may hope from God's goodness is that He will inspire my superiors to ask me to leave the seminary or novitiate. For my inability to encounter may not only destroy my own life but also damage the joy and spontaneity of those around me if I remain in the community.

Fear and insecurity may also lead to unauthentic identification. This is a movement of identification which refuses to allow for the counter-experience of self-awareness or for the discovery of my uniqueness in sameness. My only desire in this attempted encounter is in-being. I fuse my identity with the identity of my seminary director or novice mistress and never come to the sanctuary of my deepest self. Discovery of my own possibilities in the light of authentic identification is thus impossible. If I do not overcome this anxiety, I can never become a truly participative religious who is called to be a unique self-reliant witness for the Holy in the world. In this case, I do not escape into rationalism but into the identity of the other person. In my anxiety, I try to entice my superiors into a universe of emotional in-being where I welcome every chance to unburden myself to the point of exhaustion. I substitute flattery for restrained admiration and sentimental adherence for respectful love. Here again, I should be deeply grateful if the Holy Spirit illuminates my superiors so that they may unmask me before it is too late. If I am not able to transcend my problem, the best thing that can happen to me is that they would advise or even compel me to leave the novitiate. For religious life can only be torture for me and the others around me when we both discover too late my over-dependency and my uselessness as self-reliant worshipper and witness for the Lord in the culture.

The dialectics of authentic encounter are the dialectics of self-discovery. The more I identify authentically, the more I shall discover my difference from others. As soon as I deny my difference, I destroy the authenticity of encounter. Why then am I so deeply inclined to negate what I am when I meet my fellow religious? When encounter unveils me as different, anxiety may arise because to be unique entails the burden of personal responsibility, the peril of not pleasing others and therefore of being mocked and despised. Like many modern men, I too am beset by the passion to please, the need to be noticed, and the fear to be different. This demonic triad is the source of sins characteristic of communities of religious celibates. These needs incite me to identify unauthentically and to sell myself into sentimental togetherness with others which is a parody of mature love in the community. A community of participative religious would lose its meaning and usefulness in the world if it succumbed to such distorted encounter. Its purpose is to free people from a society which already distorts the inner holy orientation of its cultural and social operations under the influence of the demonic triad of the passion to please, the need to be noticed, and the fear to be different. Participative religious are called forth from this society and its familial and social establishments so that they may do battle against this distortion which easily leads to the betrayal of the objective demands of cultural-religious development. The religious community is the place where this conflict can be fought and where purification can take place. When the participative religious reenters the world thus purified he may be able to manifest his surrender to the Holy as unfolding in the culture. He will do so by participating in cultural labors in such a way that he promotes their inner aims, even if this implies his being unpopular, different, and unnoticed by the crowd.

I do not mean, of course, that the religious should be unpopular for the sake of unpopularity, unnoticed as an ideal in itself, or different for the sake of contrariness. Transcending the demonic triad and its temptations means growing toward the readiness to be unknown, displeasing, and different in the eyes of others if my worshipping and witnessing for the Holy in the culture demands or implies that I, like my Lord, become a sign of contradiction. At the moment that I am no longer willing to be a sign of contradiction rather than a crowd pleaser, I am no longer the follower of

Christ. I become meaningless and insipid and therefore deserve to be cast out and trodden upon by men.

Solitude and Recollection in the Religious Life

Community encounter implies also the development of the ability to be alone. When I dare to be myself, and to be aware of my unique call, I may experience solitude in the consciousness that I am somehow not like anyone else. As we have said, the less identification I experience, the less I know that I am different from others. Authentic identification in the active religious community leads indirectly to the opposing experience of myself as not totally identifiable, as somehow unique. It leads, therefore, to the experience of solitude which prepares me for the courage to stand alone in the world as a witness when the situation imposes this solitude on me. This very aloneness at the heart of my religious being is an opening toward the divine. There is a mysterious relationship between the experience of solitude and that of the Holy. Each religious must go through the desert of solitude in order to find God in a new way. It is then that the temptation is strongest to substitute the sentimental total in-being of an unauthentic encounter for conversion to the Holy. I must be willing to traverse the rocky plain of the lonely traveler who may feel lost and forlorn before he discovers the beauties which only the desert offers to the man who is ready to behold them.

The complementary element which pervades the dynamism of true identification and keeps it authentic is the movement of recollection. Recollection means to "gather again"; in recollection I "gather" myself before God out of the living memories of the many encounters which I have experienced up to the present time. I stand in recollection before the Holy not only in my uniqueness but also in my mode of identification. Each encounter with my fellowman brings to light some aspect of my being and helps make me aware in what way I am called to live out my potentialities in the service of the Holy. The history of my encounters is thus the partial revelation of my being as given to me up to this time of my life. The movement of identification may cause me at times to lose myself in the overwhelming "busy-ness" of social functions, conferences, and meetings. I may feel that my deepest self is slipping away and that my intimacy with the Lord is diminishing. Now the need for recollecting myself comes to the fore and permeates my need for identification with others. This is a moment of grace. It enables me to regain a prayerful presence to the Holy as revealed in my uniqueness and in the uniqueness of the other. This gathering myself in recollection prevents me from regressing to a symbiotic level of undifferentiated in-being. In recollection I come to myself — the self that I have come to know in the rich variety of encounters that I have already experienced. No one encounter reveals the all-sidedness of what I am called to be. Neither does the great variety of encounters in the past unveil exhaustively what I potentially am. Recollection is not merely a bringing back of past encounters, but a gathering of myself together in deepening the awareness of my uniqueness before God as it has grown through the various encounters in my life.

These past experiences of encounter with my fellowman are now brought together in a deeper unity in my encounter with the Holy. True encounter with the Holy roots me more deeply in my true uniqueness. This rootedness reveals at the same time the most profound meaning and reality of in-being and counter-being which I have experienced up to this moment. In my rootedness in the Holy I experience the ultimate in-being for which I am striving in all movements of identification with my fellowman. In the experience of my uniqueness granted to me by the Holy, I face the most profound meaning of counter-being after which I was unconsciously striving while recognizing, respecting, and safeguarding my identity. My deepest joy and gratitude is experienced in presence to the Holy who allows me to be a unique self called forth by Him out of nothingness and who grants me the peace of in-being in Him without being absorbed by Him. This experience helps to restore the balance between in-being and counter-being which I may have lost in my daily encounters with others. In this light the over-indulgence in identification, which at times I may have given in to, appears as treason to my uniqueness. On the other hand, the over-indulgence in counter-being appears as treason to my personal development which, denied the in-being of encounter, could not unfold wholly.

Recollection is, therefore, not a willful self-analysis. A rationalistic approach would only serve to draw me out of my intimate self and lead to a contraction of my total self into one of its small devitalized dimensions: analytical reason. No matter how important the logical attitude is for scholarship and science, it is not the stance to take when I recollect myself serenely before the Holy. Recollection is more a looking at Him than at myself. In His light I shall see who I am as mystery and who I am as revealed to myself in the variety of encounters which have been given to me. Paradoxically, the more willfully and compulsively intellectual I am in concentrating on myself, the less able I shall be to experience my uniqueness in the eyes of God. The only way to come home to myself is to remove myself from the externals of identifying encounters, to bring myself to rest, to empty my mind of preoccupation, to let go the flow of experience, to be responsive in peace to whatever the Holy allows to well up in my heart, and then to find out who I am.

Identification without recollection will destroy me as a person. Identification with the world and my cultural task, with my cultural participants and those entrusted to my care, will lessen my service to them if it is not balanced by a continual return to recollection. During my initiation into religious life, this flowing and ebbing movement of participation and recollection is actualized within the community itself. Later on, when I am sent as a religious witness in the world, the meaning of religious community takes on a different cast from what it had as a place of initiation. While the community still fosters mutual encounter among its members, it attempts to prevent their becoming so absorbed in one another as to allow no time, interest, or occasion for encounter with the cultural participants in their respective fields of activity. My increased encounter with my cultural participants necessitates that I safeguard the religious rhythm of my life by a corresponding increase in recollection and stillness before God in my religious home. This is where I return in order to gather myself again after the experience of dispersion in the world. As this return is true of my life of prayer, so it is also true of my life of study and my life of aesthetic enrichment—of recollected listening to music or silent presence to the beauty of literature and art. Therefore, my religious home should be, whenever possible, furnished with books, objects of art, and tasteful colors and designs. These foster the recollection in which my soul deepens itself so that I may return daily into the world as a man or woman of taste and graciousness.

The same need for recollection in prayer, study, and aesthetic presence is at the root of the custom of having sufficient manual help in the community. The religious witness who returns from the world for short periods of recollection should not be overburdened with chores which encroach upon the time he needs for recollected presence. If I do not experience recollection, it will be impossible for me to remain a relaxed, prayerful witness for the Holy in my cultural field of participation. I shall become the victim of unauthentic encounter because I have lost contact with the deepest sources within myself. Then my life will become meaningless. I shall soon become disgusted with religious life and perhaps long to leave it. I shall be tempted to ask myself what is the use of religious community if it loses sight of its fundamental orientation: to free me from unnecessary functional care so that I may be more available for the work of the Lord in the world; and to grant me the gift of a home to which I can retire in order to deepen myself — sometimes alone, sometimes in dialogue with others, often in quiet prayer and serene study. A participative community that burdens its religious celibates returning from their involvement in the world *primarily* with community cares, worries, and occupations has failed as a sanctuary of religious restoration. Its primary mission has been thwarted, and it may be in danger of falling prey to the final destructive force of the participative religious life: unbridled community-centeredness.

Encounter as Blessing and Affirmation of One Another

I have seen that encounter is a source of self-revelation. Some encounters make me aware of my generosity; others of my sensuality, jealousy, or aggressiveness. Others again make me conscious of an aesthetic ability I did not know existed in me, or they evoke an interest in an area of life that was dormant until encounter with a person of kindred interest awakened me to this response. My respect for the other as a unique expression of the Holy makes me bless what he is even if I cannot share his success or style of operation. Man is structured in such a way that he needs the other to say "yes" to what he is and to what he tries to accomplish. Even as a child, before he is blessed by the affirmation of the other, it is almost impossible for him to believe in the worthwhileness of what he is and does. Hence parents have to bless what is good in their children.

To bless someone's effort means to say that what he is doing is good, that it is worthwhile, that it is acceptable to God and to the community of men. This blessing relieves him from insecurity, anxiety, and the unconscious fear that in being himself he may isolate himself from the collectivity. A prehuman collectivity which is not yet a community tends toward uniformity. It begins to grow to true community only when every member becomes increasingly able to bless the unique goodness of himself and every other member. This blessing is necessary in order to counteract unauthentic guilt feelings which prevent my fellow religious and me from being ourselves. In each one of us is an unauthentic primitive guilt feeling, linked with the prepersonal belonging to a collectivity on a prehuman stage of development. In a prehuman crowd or collectivity I feel guilty when I do not blindly conform to the crowd and repress all that is truly me. In the stage of evolution in which we find ourselves today, many religious communities are torn between being such a prehuman collectivity and raising themselves to the level of true community.

One of the most effective ways to cure the religious

from the unauthentic primitive guilt which stunts his development and leads to regression into a collectivity is the repeated blessing of his uniqueness. The very possibility of religious community as community is dependent on this continual presence of mutual blessing which does not exclude respectful criticism of one another when it is needed. For respectful criticism is a blessing too or, if you will, a blessing in disguise. It is only authentic, however, when it is rooted in my willingness to help my fellow religious to be more effective, radiant, and uniquely himself as an original participant in the cultural development of mankind.

Among the greatest enemies of the celibate religious community are envy and jealousy — especially when they are masked as holy concern for the humility of fellow religious who torment others by their successful projects for the Lord. During his initiation into the religious life, everyone should be taught to recognize this hidden force which can destroy the effectiveness of community members in the world. During his entire formation, he should be made aware of this pernicious tendency that lives in each of us and that does more harm to the effective presence of religious in the world than any other fault. The tendency of the religious celibate toward jealousy is so deeply rooted and so pervades the whole of the personality that all of us try to repress awareness of it. But we must strive to unmask it, for envy and jealousy make true community encounter impossible, lead to mutual suspicion, and sometimes even prompt a religious to silent isolation in order not to evoke the demon of envy in the other. A kind of universal repression of the awareness of this cancer in religious communities can lead to a situation in which the young man or woman to be initiated is taught only about other sins, such as those against chastity, obedience, and poverty, but never about the perhaps cardinal sin of the religious celibate — the sin of jealousy and envy. It is difficult to speak about this evil because we are all tarnished by it. I may feel at ease talking about sins against the sixth and ninth commandments because, like most religious, I seldom find myself in the occasion to commit them, and I may feel small guilt concerning them. But if I enter into discussion of the secret and hidden forms of jealousy and envy, I become uneasy; the subject seems to strike home. Therefore, an honest dialogue about this vice with seminarians, novices, juniors or postulants will necessarily make us all aware that there is more envy and jealousy in us than we care to admit. I may become aghast when I begin to realize how many times I have condemned a fellow religious interiorly, if not exteriorly, in the name of concern for his virtue, while I have been really moved by an unconscious feeling of jealousy and envy. I may recall how I myself often experienced that strange little irritation when others praised a fellow religious, and how I immediately translated my irritation into a pious feeling of concern for his humility, for the purity of his motivation, for the orthodoxy of his teaching, and for the welfare of his soul. It is uncomfortable for me to face this evil in myself. Perhaps this is why many superiors, seminary directors, and novice mistresses prefer to condemn the evil of violations against chastity or poverty. With these sins I feel safe. Unfortunately, the universal repression of the awareness of the evil of jealousy that eats away at the roots of many religious communities may prevent me, when I am a religious director, from forming my students daily in this one most necessary insight.

Community encounter implies, then, the blessing of the other, the affirmation of the other, the saying "yes" to the other. Psychologically, when another blesses me I am able to make his blessing a self-blessing. I can say "yes" to myself, respect myself, have confidence in myself as rooted in the Holy. This response is the basis of self-reliant growth. In the world I shall frequently be a sign of contradiction when I do the will of the Father who sent me. My presence will not always be blessed, but frequently cursed by the crowd. I, therefore, need to experience the blessing of my efforts in my community. It is the one place in the world to which I can return to experience God's loving affirmation of me and my work through the respectful affirmation which my fellow religious grant to me.

Modes of Blessing

It may be helpful to distinguish various types of blessings which I can give in growing to true encounter with my fellow religious. Four modes are distinguishable: a fundamental and a dimensional blessing, an authentic and an unauthentic blessing. The fundamental blessing of the other occurs when I communicate to him that he is basically good, that I respect him as a person called to witness in his own way for the presence of the holy. I can and should give this respect to each community member at all times. Even if he does not always seem to live up to his calling, he still has the dignity of being called. Any criticism which I may have to communicate will thus be rooted in my respect for his true self as called forth by the Holy. Dimensional blessing, on the other hand, is the respectful affirmation of one or the other special abilities or virtues in my fellow religious. Sometimes I may not be able to grant him this gift because I may be blind to his achievement in a specific area. It would be dishonest and artificial to explode in admiration over something that has no meaning for me. In this case, I can grant my fellow religious only my fundamental respect and respectfully suspend my judgment in areas in which I am incompetent. Enjoying this fundamental affirmation, my fellow religious will not mind the absence of my affirmation in an area which he knows I do not understand.

A true blessing grows from my openness for the values in my fellow religious and my experience of them which emerges with God's grace provided my perception is not constricted by the potential envy which is within me. Unauthentic or feigned blessing is a subtle technique of seduction. I may try to seduce the other to praise me in turn, to like me, to follow me, to sustain my projects, or to form with me a mutual admiration society. In other words, my affirmation is not the honest result of openness to his worth but a clever trick to win him over. Instead of promoting his unique independence as a witness for God, I try to rob him of it. I try to steal his self-reliance by making him dependent on my approval, my praise, my flattery. A more serious type of this sin against community is to try to seduce a key person — like a superior — by flattery, praise, enthusiastic approval, or even peals of laughter over his flat jokes.

Unauthentic blessing can be detected by its exaggeration, its over-emphasis, its want of honest self-expression and criticism, especially when these may be displeasing to the person flattered. The seductive religious, who is a serious danger for the integrity of a superior, can be detected by his failure to ever express honest disagreement or dissatisfaction. It is impossible for both him and his superior to be truly themselves and still feel precisely the same about every detail of life. The line between authentic and unauthentic blessing, between affirmation of the other and seduction of the other, may be thin indeed. The mutual respect and affirmation which should be the fundamental tone in a religious community is more an attitude which reveals itself indirectly in behavior than a matter of loud verbal expression. Meals would be unbearable, for example, if the individual religious felt obligated to spend the time between courses extolling one another's virtues. More serious, however, is the fact that boisterous approval will always tempt me to be dishonest, artificial, or seductive. It is, therefore, more important to concentrate on inner attitudes of blessing than on their verbal expression.

If the right attitude is present, then it will necessarily appear in my constant respect for the privacy of the other, for his style of life, for his interest and orientation. The same respect will reveal itself in my gracious manner toward him, my scrupulous avoidance of negative criticism of his special mission, and in my absolute refusal to speak against him to my fellow religious or to outsiders. When respect is lived in this indirect way, the danger of artificiality and seduction will be absent. Moreover, direct public praise of one member may tempt fellow religious who are immature or neurotic to envy and jealousy. Also, public praise may easily become a secret weapon to enhance certain members at the expense of others. The survival of true religious spirit in a community demands that we avoid all structures which may lead to the development of distasteful community politics. The clever manipulation of public praise as a weapon of seduction and political propaganda is one of these dangerous implicit structures.

Blessing and Personal Becoming

The necessity for my unfolding as a human person and as a religious raises the question of whether I am truly free in my becoming or whether I am determined by the evaluation and blessing of others which I experience in my community encounter. If encounter and its blessing of me as a person, or of one of my dimensions of life, structured my self-appreciation in an absolute way, I would not be experiencing encounter on the human level. I would still be on the prepersonal level of encounter where there is no free meeting of two unique persons in deep mutual respect for each other's sacred individuality. On this level I would strive for a prehuman fusion dictated by anxiety and need. True encounter is an event of the spirit, a joyful celebration of each other's uniqueness and independent growth. The proof of its authenticity is the fact that I feel more free, more myself, more independent from the person whom I encounter than in any other life situation. True encounter makes me be in such a way that I feel free to express to the other that I am different. We both experience the delight of that unspeakable freedom of spirit in which we allow each other to be what we are and experience joy in each other's independence. How different this is from the sentimental, prehuman togetherness which makes us over-dependent on each other.

While I am aware that blessing is necessary for my growth, I should distinguish between a blessing which I experience as a favorable condition for self-discovery and the type of appreciation which I wrongly idolize as an ultimate criterion of self-worth. In the latter case, I am a self-alienated religious who is the puppet of the judgments and affections of others. My own self does not come into play in my behavior. My actions become disassociated from my inner self and turn into a blind performance depending upon my desire for the approval of others. This emotional in-being without counter-being gradually destroys my religious personality and renders me more or less useless for the Lord who wills to incarnate Himself in the culture through persons, not puppets. Soon I find myself caught in the flow of prehuman community excitement and gossip. Thus, restless emotional agitation replaces quiet perception and self-recollection before the Holy. As a blind conformist, I allow myself to be largely determined by the influence of others to my detriment and that of my mission in life.

In true encounter, however, the blessing of the other is experienced as a *possible* expression of the blessing of the Holy, who blesses me as His own gift. I should experience it as only a *possible partial* revelation of His blessing, for the person whom I encounter may be mistaken in his appreciation, may exaggerate my value, may try to make me dependent by disproportionate praise, or — driven by his own dependency needs — may project qualities to me which I do not possess. Moreover, if I do not receive every human blessing as only a possible participation in the blessing of the Holy, I may be tempted to react to this appreciation on the ground of pride, insecurity, or anxiety. When I do so, my human and religious self is betrayed once again.

Despite the limitations just expressed, the blessing of the other may indeed reveal to me an aspect of my personality that can be gratefully affirmed and developed with a sacred sense of obligation and faithfulness to the gifts which God has granted me. I should do this in a humble attitude of gratitude to God for His gift and avoid the self-deception that I myself am the self-sufficient source of anything that I can do or be. Otherwise, I shall live no longer in the truth, and consequently all my further self-discoveries and self-actualizations will of necessity participate in the untruth which I am living. They will lead to grotesque self-enhancement, over-sensitivity to slights, vulnerability to failure and contradiction, and a neurotic or sinful over-estimation of my personal capabilities. I shall become an unbearable member of my community and perhaps a conceited show-off in my cultural field of action. Soon I may be tempted to join forces with others, perhaps brilliant, but as conceited as I, and establish with them an exclusive mutual admiration society of persons who have chosen to live together in the untruth of self-enhancement.

The characteristics of true encounter apply not only to the authentic meeting of persons in the community but also to the interaction of each person and the community as a whole. In the beginning of my encounter with the community, the experience of inbeing may prevail. It is even possible that this aspect or pole of encounter may become so exclusive that I do not experience the community as community, but as a crowd or collectivity in which I blindly submerse my personality. Grace may help me to go beyond this stage and to "face" my community as a person, unique and different. This is the beginning of my growth to true community life. Now the counter-experience may be predominant. This temporary experience may become so exclusive that I do not have community experience at all, but the experience of a self that is in no way related to the other. In this period I lose my prepersonal fusion with those with whom I experienced submergence in a blind crowd or collectivity, but I do not yet feel able to develop a true personal encounter. In the beginning of this new experience of selfhood, I fear to fall back again into the faceless collectivity from which I have emerged so painfully. I find myself suspended between the safe experience of conformity and the need to safeguard my newly discovered self. This crisis is a gift of the Holy which may lead to my birth as a true member of the community if I am faithful to God's grace.

My birth as a self-reliant community member is a fascinating process. In some respects, it can be clarified by my insight into the first stirrings of the child on a similar, but lower level of development. This insight may help me to discover which conditions in the religious community are conducive to the growth of its members beyond the stage of collectivity. The occasion on which the child first discovers himself as a somewhat independent entity is his experience of having a secret. Before that moment, the child is not aware of the fundamental possibility of developing an inner life of his own. He does not yet realize that his thoughts, perceptions, and emotions are not totally open to the people who surround him. He lives in-being so fully with his mother that he feels as if she shares his every thought and emotion. When he discovers for the first time that she does not know a thought he is thinking, a feeling he is experiencing, or something he has done without her knowledge, he experiences surprise and elation. He is overwhelmed by the awareness that in some way he is on his own and escapes the all-powerful, all-present, and all-knowing grown-ups around him. He exalts in the awareness of his new power, the power to admit his mother into his hidden feeling, thought, or action, or to exclude her by keeping it secret. The experience of having a secret is one of the most decisive experiences of life, for the secret that I have symbolizes the secret that I am.

This function of the secret, or at least of the respected possibility of and right to a secret, plays a similar role in the life of the adult and in the society of adults. In having a secret I become aware that I am a secret, a mystery for others and for myself. Being an incarnated spirit, I need a concrete embodiment of my spiritual uniqueness and of the respect due to this uniqueness by all. This embodiment can be found in the respect for my privacy as embodied in concrete structures and customs of the religious community, and in the attitudes and behaviors of its superiors and members. It is almost impossible for a human collectivity to grow toward a religious community without this continual respect for the sacred privacy of each member, who is encouraged to maintain an inner dimension of holy secrecy which fosters his dignity and self-respect as a religious person. A community in which everyone is devoured by the need to know everything about everyone else is a crowd of childish people who have to relieve themselves constantly of what they think and feel. They experience a tortured anxiety when faced with the self-withholding dignity of a fellow religious who does not feel the same childish compulsion to pour all his thoughts into the void of a gossipy crowd.

The participative religious community, therefore, as a home for the formation of self-reliant witnesses to the Holy, fosters customs and structures which promote the dignity and privacy of all. Letters should remain unopened, telephone calls unchecked; prying into the personal relationships of the religious with his family members, friends, and acquaintances in the field of his cultural endeavors should be avoided. To be sure, we do not deny the religious community the right and duty to protect itself against serious damage which a member who is mentally ill or morally malicious may inflict. But such damage is the exception, not the rule. When a fellow member is absent, no one should disrespectfully inquire where he is or what he is doing. Practicing contrary customs will make it difficult for the average religious to encounter people inside and outside the community in a mature way.

It is impossible for the average person to grow to a dignified and impressive self-possession if he feels that his comings and goings are potentially exposed to the eyes and ears of all. The men who organized concentration camps were deeply aware of this psychological truth. They went so far as to mastermind a system in which external privacy and secrecy were totally diminished in order to dehumanize the inmates. We know that their project succeeded all too well, at least among the average prisoners whose dignity, strength, and self-reliance were soon broken by the system. The authentic religious community masterminds the opposite development. It offers a structure of such protection and promotion of the sacred privacy of each religious that it elevates the average man or woman to a mature dignity and self-reliance which make him or her a splendid revelation of the Lord when entering the field of culture as an accomplished personality.

CONCLUSION

Culture And Religious Life In A Time Of Transition

Participative religious life is not only a question for the individual religious and his community but for the whole culture as well. The culture first of all generously encourages some of its best youth to serve the Holy in this life. Then the participative religious, after his spiritual metamorphosis, is called to reenter the culture as a witness for the sacred dimension of culture itself. In other words, the participative religious life comes from the culture and returns to it, affecting its orientation at least as a constant reminder of its own deepest ground.

Culture and religious life are so deeply interwoven that the increase or decrease of religious vocations parallels the increase or decrease of the cultural or subcultural estimation of this life. The average child develops his appreciation of the various states of life in accordance with the evaluations which prevail in his surroundings. When fathers and mothers, teachers and clergymen, schools and families, intellectuals and artists lose their sensitivity to the central values of religious life within the culture, they can no longer radiate respect for this calling among the young. As a result, fewer feel attracted to it. They seldom stop to consider that many question this life because they find fault with its accidental features. They should become aware of the essential historical meaning and value of religious life before they foolishly reject it on the basis of aberrations in temporary and local features. To those for whom religion is a matter of externals, a mere humanism or moral behaviorism, religious life will remain a closed book. Those people, however, who truly try to live in presence to the Holy may sense the inner orientation and cultural importance of religious life in spite of certain features no longer, or not yet, in tune with the essential meaning of religious life. Those truly spiritual people who feel in doubt about the desirability of religious life may experience a conflict of conscience. They may ask themselves: Can I please God if I do not respect and promote this special life of religious presence?

The questioning of religious life is as prevalent among non-religious as among religious. I as an individual may be called to religious life, but it is the culture which in a profound sense is called to set me and others free for this mode of presence. The culture honors itself by allowing me and others to represent and symbolize the value of cultural-religious presence, so that it too may profit from my life specialization by remaining more open to its own most fundamental ground.

No wonder the culture asks itself whether it should promote in its midst the specialization of a life that may deeply influence the flow of its motivation and intention. The members of participative religious orders do not restrict their life of worship and witness to the enclosure of community and convent, but demonstrate in the world itself how to live one's cultural involvement in a religious way. When the world is permeated by large groups of religious witnesses, the spiritual style of the culture is necessarily affected by their presence. When people choose to foster the emergence of religious life in their midst, they choose a certain influence on their own life as sacred. It was interesting to observe, for example, the reactions of certain Protestants to the emergence of Protestant religious life, such as that exemplified in the monastery of Taize. Some of them were adverse to it because they felt that universal enthusiastic support by Protestantism might lead not only to a powerful emergence of Protestant religious life but also to a change in Protestantism itself. They were right. No subculture can free some of its best sons and daughters for religious worship and witness without being influenced later by the religious powers which it has liberated. This is more fundamentally true of specialization in religious presence than of any other concentration in cultural values, whether aesthetic, scientific, or humanistic. For the specialization of groups of witnesses for the Holy in any culture is the most fundamental ground of the very possibility of balanced cultural, social, and technical achievements by all.

If the emergence of religious existence and its wholesome and effective development are so crucial for the maintenance and growth of my culture, the questions surrounding this life cannot leave unmoved my fellowmen who are so passionately concerned about the highest possible humanization of man. I should not be surprised by the burning, sometimes critical attention centered upon the men or women who are called to guard and promote the highest possible openness for that value of the culture which is the stimulus to a balanced and creative unfolding of all other values. I should welcome this interest and listen serenely to criticism, even when it is unreasonable, lopsided, and the bitter fruit of prejudice, misconception, and traumatic experiences in the meeting with organized religion. I should also understand why various scholars, artists, and scientists who are not affiliated with any form of organized religion, may still show interest in the religious life. They may sense intuitively that the inner orientation of religious life is to foster the religious attitude in all mankind as engaged in the evolvement of the world. They may hope that the specialists in religious openness and experience whom they encounter in all fields of art, science, and social endeavor may communicate to them how to live in openness to the Holy, which alone can make life livable and meaningful in the deepest sense. They may be deeply interested in the men and women who go out from religious communities to baptize every dimension of the culture by their very life of religious presence. Striving for religious openness outside organized religion, they may seek for illumination in my silent life of worship and witness for the Holy, since I live among them and participate wholeheartedly in their daily cultural endeavors.

I must expect that the questioning from inside and outside religious life will not leave me untouched. At least initially it may lead to insecurity, depression, and anxiety. I may well doubt the very meaning of my religious life, overwhelmed as I am by the onslaught of debasing remarks aimed at it from all sides. Reflecting on the doubts evoked in me by this opposition, I may discover that I have chosen the religious life partly on false premises. This discovery is a gift, for it will enable me to purify my motivations. The motivations for every state of life are always complex and mixed. While the core of human motivation may be inspired by the central values to be realized in one or the other state of life, this core is usually surrounded by a confusion of other motivations somehow interwoven with the main motivation. True human growth in any state of life means an increasing purification of the motivations for this state under the impact of life experience and the gift of suffering, which cleanses away the fantasies and illusions clouding the simple and straight direction. The call to the religious life does not escape the law of motivational development. According to this law, a fundamental life motivation can grow in purity only in the course of experience and suffering.

If the questioning of society disrupts a false security, this is a beneficial disruption which can help me to purify my motivations and to root my security anew in the real meaning and value of the religious life. My early years may have been spent in a subculture in which religious life had attained such a position of honor and influence that it was valued not only for its inner meaning but also for its social status, economic security, and popularity among the people. Such extrinsic advantages of religious life, such secondary gains in certain subcultures or in certain cultural periods, are by no means to be deprecated. When the Holy in certain periods and locations of its historical unfolding grants such secondary gains, I should gratefully accept and enjoy them. Secondary gains or losses accompany all primary life situations. However, my daily personal experience of security is inevitably influenced by these secondary social factors. A problem arises when such accidental grounds of security and self-esteem change during my lifetime, which is precisely what happens historically when I am called to live in a time of transition. As a religious in a time of cultural and social transition, I may experience that the accidental and secondary grounds of my security and self-esteem are fading away. I may also realize to my surprise that such secondary aspects played a greater role in my security system than I consciously realized. I may experience panic and become almost neurotically defensive over the loss of these accidental conditions of security. I may feel as if my very existence as a religious is in jeopardy. I shall experience this response most dramatically if my personal security was rooted more in the secondary benefits of religious life than in the primary ground of religious security, which is my lived intimacy with the Holy.

The same is true of my religious community. Human communities as well as individuals develop security systems and self-appreciations which are rooted sometimes in secondary conditions. Therefore, the religious community as a whole may also experience panic in a period of transition. Like the individual religious, the community too must then root itself more deeply in the primary ground of security in religious life, while at the same time becoming less dependent on the secondary grounds of security.

Questioning and Commitment

Today I may experience in concrete ways that the high social estimation in which religious life was held when I entered my community has given way to a temporary depreciation. It may be difficult for me to live this life in serenity when almost everyone around me seems to question its value. Actually, I am in an ideal situation to become maturely independent of such superficial factors as popular respect or the acclaim of the crowd. I may now open myself to the mysterious ground of unshakable certainty in the religious vocation, which is simply the inner call of the Lord in my personal life. Even if it were true that married life, for example, would make me happier and more mature, I would not desire it because my Lord has not called me to it. It is as simple as that. To be called by the Lord and to follow His call is the deepest duty of each Christian no matter in what state of life, and in spite of the consequences of this faithfulness.

Choosing to respond to this deep inclination in the core of my being was a personal decision. Maybe I have never made this decision explicit. If this is so, then the grace of questioning religious life is that it may compel me to make explicit my fundamental choice, which until now has been covered by layers of secondary motivations. Without this conscious fundamental decision, no life can be lived dynamically, wholeheartedly, and to the full. Moreover, this basic option is necessary for the development of my ability to respond rightly to the questions posed about my religious existence.

A fundamental and lasting commitment is in itself a mode of presence to the reality of life. I mean that each commitment itself opens up a corresponding realm of insight and understanding that would remain closed without it. For example, if I commit myself to a marriage partner for a lifetime, the light of this commitment itself will reveal to me many ways to overcome the crises in our life of mutual commitment. On the other hand, if I should say to my partner, "I desire to live with you for a few years, and then we shall decide whether or not to continue," the chances that our relationship would be broken before the time of decision are greater than if I should commit myself fundamentally once and for all. In the same way, my fundamental commitment to religious life grants me a way to deal with my crises within this life, a way which would be withheld from me if I were not truly committed. Therefore, I can never completely trust the judgments of a religious who is not yet, or no longer, fundamentally committed to this life. He lacks the most important source of enlightenment: unconditional commitment to his call.

The light of my primary decision or my fundamental commitment should guide my questioning of religious life. It would be incorrect to expect, however, that this light will be mine only when my commitment is based on the certainty of the scientific laboratory or the electronic computer. No personal life decision can be rooted in such certitude. If I were to commit myself to a marriage partner only on the scientifically guaranteed calculation that we would be perfectly successful and happy in our married life, of course I would never marry. In matters of personal life, there is never a predictable certitude of success and happiness. The personal life decision is a leap into the darkness of not totally knowing. It is taking a risk. It is a religious act of trust in the Lord. The meaningfulness of man's life depends on the wholeheartedness of the leap and its continuation. Even when I have made my fundamental decision, I should renew and deepen this decision at various periods of my life. Each renewal should imply an incarnation of my later experiences of insight, joy, and suffering, each of which reveals my chosen life to me under new aspects. In marriage, for example, a crisis of misunderstanding, the loss of a child, economic difficulties, prolonged illness, incapacitation of the marriage partner, temporary unfaithfulness to each other — all are situations which call for a renewed and deepened decision. The same is true of religious life. Therefore, I may become a far better religious in a time of questioning, turmoil, and transition than in a time of peace when I would have enjoyed the unquestioned continuation of the many secondary benefits supporting my security system.

The Predicament of Moses

In a period of transition and questioning, there arises what I like to call the predicament of Moses. All people who live in a time of transition are able, like Moses, to see a glimpse of the Promised Land, but at the same time know like him that they may never enter it personally. Religious in a time of transition may be called to dwell in the desert for a lifetime with a chosen but at the same time disgruntled, complaining people. They may have glimpses of the Promised Land of a renewed religious life, but they may also realize that they will not live long enough to enjoy it themselves. If I do not accept this position in history in relaxed and prayerful surrender, I may develop into an anxious, angry, disgruntled religious who feels cheated because he has not been called to live in an earlier or later period of history.

As a religious living in the present time, I must sooner or later come to terms with the historical destiny which I share with my generation. There is no way out. I cannot choose my time to be born and my time to die. As long as I cannot accept wholeheartedly the unavoidable historical dimension of my existence, it will be impossible for me to live in serenity. I shall not be able to reach the full effectiveness which I could reach if my energy and emotionality were not being continually drained by unconscious opposition to my historical destiny. This surrender to my destiny as a religious in a time of transition is possible only when, with God's grace, I develop a deep and abiding faith that every season is God's season — that every period of the historical unfolding of the Holy is a good period in His mysterious project which spreads itself out over all generations. I can find joy and happiness in my existence only when I try to be faithful to the limited task allotted to me by the Holy in this mysterious project.

Again, such commitment is a necessary condition for meaningful answers to the questions about religious life as they are posed at this time. They will be humble answers in which I shall try with my generation to achieve the limited aims which the development of history asks us to bear. I shall neither underestimate nor overestimate the value of my answers. I shall not make my peace and joy dependent on the expectation that we shall find final answers. The source of my joy is not that I am the religious who knows all the answers, but that I try to be faithful to the Holy. To be in accord with the Divine Will and to be intimate with the unfolding of history are the ground of boundless joy and optimism, even if my answers are proved awkward and incomplete by the next generation.

The questioning of religious life is not isolated, therefore, from the hidden dynamics of the cultural period in which I am living, nor from the fundamental presence to reality which the human being is. Man as an embodied spirit is called to be religiously present to the Transcendent in and through immediate appearances in his surroundings. Man is a fundamental tension between these two forces which constitute his very being. At the present moment of history mankind lives in a one-sided concentration on immediate appearances. Ours is a period in which the goodness, truth, and beauty of the immediate reveal themselves more strikingly than ever before to the astonished eyes of mankind. Science, art, and technique penetrate increasingly into the powers and possibilities of man and matter. They conspire to make available to us all that reality in its immediacy has to offer for our self-fulfillment. The whole of mankind seems to be involved in a gigantic experiment to find out to what degree the human being can find fulfillment by the use of the unbelievable treasures discovered in immediate reality. Our age is the age of testing the limits. Man is testing the boundaries of fulfillment possible in a life lived exclusively in presence to the treasures made available by science, medicine, art, and the dynamics of psychology. We witness a frantic attempt to try out the possibilities of modern housing and travel, of increased physical and psychological health and vigor, of beautification of the body, of sexuality, of the achievement and preservation of an agreeable personality. This overemphasis is necessarily accompanied by an increasing neglect of the other more fundamental need in man, the need for the Transcendent, or what can be called his fundamental religious need. The psychology of man teaches us that the repression of a fundamental need does not destroy it but, on the contrary, makes it more powerful and potentially explosive. The longer a basic need in man is frustrated, the greater its outburst will be. The neglected need for the transcendent will emerge in awareness when the period of testing the limits comes to its natural end — when mankind finds these limits and realizes that immediacy, even in its most fulfilling features, cannot satisfy him. Usually, the end of such a period is accompanied by increasing restlessness, dissatisfaction, neurosis, fear, and anxiety. Other symptoms may be a sudden eruption of exotic cults and the use of intoxicants which can liberate man from the pressure of immediacy and its demands.

These manifestations are the prelude of an age of religion. However, an age of religion that follows upon an age of testing the limits has to be lived by a population which not only is hungry for presence to the Transcendent, but also has learned to appreciate the limited, but real values of immediate activities and appearances. In other words, the explosion of the need for religion which is bound to come will lead to a search for a presence to the Holy which can be integrated with the continuation of an unfolding of the truth of the immediate. But the latter will then be experienced as a gift and challenge of the Holy. Thus, there will be a tremendous need, perhaps unparalleled in history, for people who specialize in presence to the Transcendent or to the religious dimension of cultural activities.

We believe that the participative religious communities are essentially oriented toward the fostering of such witnesses in the culture. We foresee that the inner dynamics of history will force the participative religious communities to come into their own for the first time in history. We foresee a springtime of participative religious communities whose members will permeate the culture in a new and inspiring way. The same historical dynamics are already operating among us today in the on-going questioning of the meaning and structures of religious life. The age to come reveals itself already in our anxious concern with the relevance of religious life for our times. Even if we are not called to live in the coming age of religious synthesis and integration, we are called to question our religious life now in order to prepare for its fundamental task in the centuries to come.